POEMS TO NAVIGATE CARIBBEAN DIASPORA DISRUPTIONS

By

ROSELLE THOMPSON

EAGLE PUBLICATIONS

Published by Eagle Publications
P O Box 73374, London W3 3FZ, England.
A Paperback Original
First published in the United Kingdom in 2021

Text copyright © 2021 Roselle Thompson
The right of Roselle Thompson to be identified as the Author
of this work has been asserted by her.

ISBN 978-1-8381068-5-0
A CIP catalogue record for this book is available from the
British Library
All Rights Reserved

This book is sold subject to the condition that it shall not, by way of trade or otherwise, be lent, hired out or otherwise circulated in any form of binding or cover other than that in which it is published. No part of this publication may be reproduced, stored in a retrieval system, or transmitted in any form or by any means (electronic, mechanical, photocopying, recording or otherwise) without the prior written permission of Eagle Publications.

All paper used by Eagle Publications is SFI (Sustainable Forestry Initiative) and PEFC (Programme for the Endorsement of Forest Certification Schemes) Certified.

This is a work of fiction. Names, characters, incidents, and dialogues are products of the author's imagination or are used fictitiously. Any resemblance to actual people, living or dead, events or locales is entirely coincidental.

Printed in the United Kingdom and United States by
Lightning Source for Eagle Publishers

www.eaglepublications.org.uk

CONTENTS

Introduction		i-x
1.	Echoes of Memory	1
2.	Tropical Sunrise Sea	3
3.	The Gift of Flowers	5
4.	Words are Bullets	7
5.	The Old Pub	8
6.	Natural Woman	10
7.	Borders and Boundaries	12
8.	Education Fail	13
9.	Elvira's Soul	14
10.	Song of the Caged Bird	16
11.	Migrants Sing the Blues	18
12.	Grand Etang Lake	19
13.	Doh tek yuh eyes an' pass meh!	21
14.	I Fell into Heaven	23
15.	Black Writers	24
16.	Windrush Betrayal	26
17.	*The Talk:* Mantra for Keeping Black Children Alive	28
18.	Paradise	32
19.	COVID-19 Directives 2020!	34
20.	Still Birth	35
21.	Loki's Return	37
22.	May their Living Souls *RIP*	38
23.	Motherland Dramas	40
24.	Rejection to Influence	41
25.	Rich Man, Poor Man, Beggar Man, Thief!	43

26. Soucouyant Bite Me!	45
27. Ciara's Costly Catastrophe	47
28. Ode to the Sun	49
29. The Broken Clay Pot	50
30. A Bright Shining Star	51
31. The Enemy Within	52
32. Wedding Picture	54
33. The World is not Enough	56
34. Our Village	58
35. A Voice of Our Own	60
36. Trauma Begets Trauma	64
37. Somebody Great	66
38. I Saw a Ghost	67
39. Diversity	68
40. Go on, Laugh!	70
41. Reality Hits Home!	71
42. The Fear of Returning	73
43. When the words just won't come	76
44. 'Death' Does Not Become Her	77
45. Just Come!	79
46. Working Woman	80
47. Blessings	81
48. Imagine This!	82
49. The Breeze Calls	83
50. Vive Le Spirit Anancy: The Bridge-Builder!	84
Glossary	86

INTRODUCTION

The title of this Collection, *Poems to Navigate Caribbean Diaspora Disruptions*, suggests two major events have taken place in the lives of Caribbean people. The first is that they have migrated from their former landscape (the Caribbean region), and have settled in foreign places which categorise them as being 'in the Diaspora.' This physical movement away from a "centre," results in disruptions and cultural shifts, in a migrant's life, with myriad consequences. For example, one consequence is the need to hold tenaciously onto memories of the past - personal and collective, to help dispel traumatic experiences in the Diaspora. These can range from migrants feeling alienated in their chosen host countries, to experiences of systematic racism, discrimination, and socio-economic exclusion.

Such migrants are called Diasporeans, because the word "*diaspora*" comes from the Greek verb *'speiro,'* which means "to scatter" and the preposition *'dia,'* which means "over." Therefore, the word *'Diaspora'* refers to the dispersion or scattering of Caribbean people from the Caribbean region, to two or more peripheral places such as UK, USA, and Canada; places where Caribbean migrants have settled and have replicated their cultural traditions over time. An explicit example of this is the annual West Indian Carnival in Notting Hill, West London; now regarded or rebranded by many as, *'Europe's biggest street festival.'*

Diasporic culture involves socio-economic, political, and cultural transnational exchanges, among the separated populations of the Diaspora. However, all is not plain sailing, and it often means that these migrants undergo challenges that necessitate invoking and duplicating their culture, (as they project semblances of life in their *'back home'* countries); as part of their coping strategies in the Diaspora. Therefore, Diasporic spaces have a multitude of cultural representations that can empower, and at other times, also disempower the migrant.

For those like myself, who have migrated to the UK, Caribbean Diasporic settlements, located in and around the UK, can now be seen as integral and inseparable parts of the fabric of British society; its culture as well as its literature. Consequently, we can agree that Caribbean writers have made a substantial contribution to both Caribbean and Black British literatures; the fact that these expatriates represent both cultures whilst living in the one location. Given that such writings occupy a very significant position between both countries, they simultaneously generate theories and define positions, as they construct and reconstruct a new identity in the host country. Within this creative/recreative process, are embodied culture and traditions that have internalised nostalgia and project memory as empowerment in their survival strategies. This is because the migrant physically and psychologically occupy two spaces, which create a sense of being "*in between*" cultures, locations, and nations. This space, which is outside of 'borders,' interrogates issues to do with their development from their Caribbean landscape, and its impact on their lives in England. Therefore, Caribbean migrant writers also occupy two societies, in spatial metaphors that identify them as being between places, borders, and boundaries, and often living on the margins of their host countries. Consequently, this makes it impossible to ignore the inter-connectedness of both spaces and the significance of these, in defining their sense of *Self* or *Identity;* as they negotiate disruptions that affect their settled lives in the Diaspora.

Memory as a Coping Strategy in the Diaspora

In this Collection of poems, **memory, or the act of remembering,** is presented as an essential factor for migrants, in their practical approach to ensuring they understand, and project life as previously lived in the Caribbean, (and its value to *memory*), in aspects of their Diasporic life. As the writer of this Collection, being a Grenadian, engages a dominant Grenadian sentiment in memory recall. This can be seen especially in the poems which present the Grenadian landscape, and the part played by *memory*, in transmitting this knowledge to readers; as seen in poems such as, **Grand Etang Lake**, **The Village** and **Paradise;** which are actual physical places in Grenada.

Additionally, the process of memory formation and recollection as seen in the poem, **A Voice of Our Own**, portray subjects that deal with

ancestral linkages, via its historical content, elucidates how Caribbean languages took shape and developed from pre-Columbian, colonization, post-colonial periods, to present day; with projected characteristics of self-determination and sacrifice; are endorsed as necessary recollection in re-shaping identity. Despite the events of disrupted language acquisitions, the poem suggests there are also positive memory formations that make for happy recollection and redirection of society.

In contrast, the poem *"Still Birth,"* presents an unpleasant group memory, of the region's historical landscape, through the voice of an unborn foetus, which chooses not to be born into a life of slavery, by wielding the only power it has in its pre-birth stage; denying its potential colonial owner power over him, by choosing to die. This poem is a dramatic monologue, where the foetus is intuitively thinking about the future, having analysed the present and past conditions of its potential parents, and decides not to be born alive. The foetus, as poetic voice, is presented as knowledgeable that a live birth will not give it the freedom to live as an unshackled slave; in a world where life is projected as hellish, with incessant suffering. The foetus understands the intricacies of life already lived by its ancestors and, as unsettling as it is to read, its sensitivity to the potential horrors awaiting its birth, is firmly rooted in a reality that is based on facts.

The poem assesses the turmoil and danger of life in the world it is likely to enter and concludes that its live birth would be counter-productive or daunting; hence, its negative tone of choosing death over life. The poem is definitely not meant to be negative towards life in general, but to capture the fears and anxieties mirrored in adults of its time; potential parents, as well as generations who have experienced the ill fate which the foetus is describing. Positively, the foetus can be seen as excercising its "freedom," self-determination, or own free-will, in choosing its fate; instead of participating in the horrors it would face, being born on a slave plantation. This is compared to living in a servile world where choice is non-existent or definitely never an option.

As a result, the poetic voice could be seen positively, as the voice of an "ancestral warrior," in rebellion or revenge, against a dominant servile existence; and thus able to halt the perpetuation of systems of slavery, in ways that slaves themselves had no power or choice to do.

Similarly, migrating to England and experiencing the differences between the two landscapes, have presented opportunities for migrants to portray a wellspring of reflection, imagination, recollection of experiences in the Diaspora. These vary across a wide spectrum and can be seen in *The Fear of Returning*, where the migrant is in denial of accepting the practicality of the aging process, and its challenges for the Caribbean returnee's dilemma of having to live, without the customary social care, received by migrants in the Diaspora. In contrast, *Motherland Dramas*, portrays the dilemma of remaining in the Diaspora with its complexity and daily challenges, and project characteristics of tenacity and "re-claiming" the *right to remain* in the British-Caribbean Diaspora, with justifications for a Caribbean diasporic presence in the UK.

In poems such as *Windrush Betrayal* and *Rejection to Influence*, a range of emotions is evoked – at times tension, regret, nostalgia, and anger. These are interrogated as shown by settled migrants, in response to the political expulsion of former 'Windrush' migrants, (so called, having arrived in the UK on the HMS Empire Windrush in 1948); some of whom were later deported illegally from the UK. In *Rejection to Influence*, this poem documents the rise of Black-led churches in Britain, historicizing their journey from initial rejection in 1950's Britain, to later acceptance; once the religious, socio-economic and cultural benefits to society became apparent to the host country. These poems document the experiences of migrants in the Caribbean Diaspora in the UK, by portraying the challenging experiences migrants face, but at times they also present their many triumphs, whilst negotiating life in Britain.

Memory as a survival strategy or coping mechanism from a Grenadian migrant's perspective, is also projected on several levels in this Collection as follows:

- **Memory as recollection** of events from the past. In some cases, past events come back to haunt us, or happy memories help to brighten our days and lift our spirits from sadness or moments of despair; *(Personal and group)*. This is reflected in poems such as, *The Breeze Calls, Echoes of Memory,* and *Tropical Sunrise Sea.*

- **Memory which helps to define our sense of self and distinguishes who we are**; especially our strength of character, as distinct from others, is seen in *A Natural Woman* and *Doh Tek yuh eyes an' pass meh! Song of the Caged Bird* and *Working Woman;* which connect the place which shaped our sense of self and belonging, to the present. *(Personal memory)*

- **Memory of collective activities and gatherings of people.** For example, poems which adopt the storytelling tradition and transmit cultural wisdom, are *Soucouyant Bite Me! Elvira's Soul,* and *Vive Le Spirit Anancy: The Bridge-Builder.* In other words, memory has a social role, as it helps to shape and preserve our traditions and sense of belonging to a community, through our shared cultural experiences. *(Group memory)*

- **Cultural memory** also plays a specific role in reflecting our cultural make-up and becomes the template through which we define ourselves; wherever we are located around the globe. Therefore, cultural memories are not static, but are also formed by socio-economic, political, historical, and present experiences, of migrants in the Diaspora. These therefore highlight the complexity of *memory*; as it can inspire a range of emotions so clearly, that it cannot be one single thing.

- **Memory's role in directing/re-directing society,** can be instrumental in imparting knowledge, via their rhetorical standpoint; seen in poems such as, *Migrant Sings the Blues, Diversity, Black Writers* and *Education Fail,* although the entire Collection embodies these characteristics.

Given the above perspectives, it is possible to conclude that *memory* establishes a feeling of nostalgia in the text, and it is used as a method of exploring both individual and cultural identity. Therefore, it invites us to reflect on both sorrow and triumph; meaning, when we remember sad events, it acts as a reminder of how we suffered loss. For some, that loss can be softened over time and for those who are unable to cope with its complexity, it causes pathological behavior that can be equally troubling. But the act of remembering can also create opportunities for the relief of sadness and enable us to feel triumphant. These perspectives confirm that we have the capacity to carry the past within us, wherever we go, and as a result, it can be resurrected at intervals; based on circumstances that trigger emotions, giving rise to specific memories.

For example, *group/collective memory* is alluded to in the poem *Education fail*. In this poem, the poetic voice references 'group' customs, by focusing on a cultural tradition that is distinctly Caribbean; the creation of *Su-su*. This is one of the oldest forms of folk banking performed by villagers, which involve one person who is elected to collect a specified sum of money from several people who form a group. Pooling their money on a weekly/monthly basis, the total sum collected is given, in turn, to each member of the group, in a circular formation, until everyone has had a turn. It is called "*Pardner*" in Jamaica, "*a Hand*" in other parts of the Caribbean, and "*Conubite*" in Haiti/Latin America. The allusion to *Su-Su* in the poem presents the irony that the simplicity and effectiveness of such a group/collective initiative, is immediately lost to 'educated' citizens in society, who dismissing its efficacy, believe that "betterment" is to be found in developed metropolitan cities, abroad, in the Diaspora; only to discover later that this was illusory.

As a result, it is also possible to view the reality of the migrants' experiences as being tied up with a sense of *loss*, which can be interpreted on the following levels: *loss* of cultural identity and having to embrace a foreign culture; *loss* of self-worth, seen in their disappointment, engendered by being branded as "inferior "within the host community; *loss* of a shared identity - having to grapple with repeated changes to their identity in England.

A case in point is the recent political actions in the UK, where Caribbean migrants of the early 1950s were eventually categorized as identity-less, after 60 years of settlement in the UK, as seen in the poem *Windrush Betrayal*. The reality of *loss* of an inherited status, to feelings of marginalization, and rejection imposed by the British government's actions have undermined a sense of belonging or allegiance to Britain; caused in this case, by the illegal deportations of Caribbean Migrants. Consequently, there is an issue that the former colonized migrant is now forced to recognize that Britain or other Metropolitan cities in the West, once seen as the citadels of advancement and the 'only' means to socio-economic progress, as a misconceived ideal; this issue is also explored here in poems such as, *Education Fail*, and *Migrant Sings the Blues*. Other subjects in this Collection, such as *The Talk: Mantra for Keeping Black Youths Alive*, and *Rejection to Influence* were influenced by extensive research done among the Caribbean diaspora community in Britain, during the production of a weekly TV documentary series on the *Roselle & Friends Talk Show*, that highlighted the day-to-day experiences and survival strategies employed by Caribbean migrants in the Diaspora. The findings confirm their continuing and historic existence in Britain; as being part of the fabric of British society; for better or worse.

  This Collection, *Poems to Navigate Caribbean Diaspora Disruptions*, also raises important issues about the relationship between personal experience, the selected medium of presenting these, and choice of poems included. In fact, within the Collection we can see how different levels of remembering and the impact this has in each poem, seem to suggest that some issues linked to a person's *memory*, can compete for recognition for different reasons; ultimately it confirms that *memory* is selective and as such, can present some complexities for Diasporeans. Therefore, I make my intentions clear, by stating some of the intricacies explored, when writing the poems in this Collection.

  Firstly, the structural dominance of the poems is free verse, because I believe free verse enforces any form of structure and replicates experiences at its simplest. I've also experimented with various poetic forms, such as the *Villanelle, Calligram, Strophe*, use of *Grenadian dialect* and my most novel experimentation yet, is the poem entitled *Imagine This!* The structural device of this poem presents lines that are interposed with an extensive use of / (*the slash or virgule*), to show line breaks between single words and phrases. This is to heighten the rhythm and to express an imaginative interpretation of the subject as an interrupted monologue. Each word resonates to form sonic cues that make the poem read differently, e.g. conveys aesthetic or emotional qualities, so that sound is mediating the interaction, rather like a Rapper, allowing for addition of meanings – as he/she wraps the words around and shouts it out all in one go; with no room for surprise. Writing this poem was an aural experience; I heard the rhythm first, then I wrote the poem!

Overall, the poems are reflective of the exultation of the moment of memory recall and realisation. It's important to note that the poems which respect, and reflect the past, rejoice in that moment and have implications for the future. This is because the past is gone, the present moment is important, as it reveals some repercussions in this temporal existence, with an unknown future. Therefore, poetry becomes a philosophy which conveys ideas that share with us their connectedness to all aspects of life; past, present, and future. The poems of this Collection also address the reader personally, and question their own views on issues presented, whilst projecting certain truths that may be caught up in general socio-political and historical concealment.

Consequently, this makes poetry a silent transaction of thoughts or an exchange of views. In other words, it is both expression (for the poet), and experience (for the reader). Moreover, I believe poetry should penetrate the surface, and delve beyond it, into the hidden core of things, in order to emulate realities, and reveal the unseen spectre, to the less sensitive. From this perspective, it would be true to say that words of poetry should not merely please, but present a union, from which the reader gleans the essence of issues presented by the poet. However, philosophy apart, poetry can also serve as a record of life, where mortal memories are immortalised; fixed in words, as is done in this Collection.

Memory then, is based on observations of subjects caught in their moment, which sensitizes the migrant to many things such as; smells, the food, the breeze, rainfall, (and the smell of it, after strong sunshine), music, people, the market, the landscape, etc; all are reminders which help to maintain a cultural link that confirms you came from somewhere, and belonged there; yet also belong here, in the Diaspora; as captured succinctly in the poem, *Echoes of Memory*. Notwithstanding, cultural representation can, at times, seem almost insignificant as the dream in the poem, *I Saw A Ghost;* but it is celebrated because it has meaning that is crucial to migrants, away from their homeland. In other words, nothing is forgotten for the migrant who clings on to every aspect of life experienced '*back home;*' insisting that everything should be remembered. In some cases, this provides the motivation for living in the Diaspora, when times become tough or unbearable. I believe these lyrical presentations carve their own place in history for the ordinary man, woman, and child; making what was once temporal, a more permanent lifeline for survival.

Moreover, this Collection of poems present an avenue for the subjects that are brushed aside by those who regard poetry as a medium for the elite, the noble, the glorious and conquerors. In subverting such notions, and redressing the balance, I invite the reader, as expressed in the poem, *Rich man, Poor man, Beggar man, Thief!* to consider the point being made - that in certain circumstances, there are no real differences among them. It is also a truism which suggests there is no difference between the subject matter of poems that are in praise of the nobility, and those of the slave, the slain, or those relegated to the periphery by society; as not having poetic merit. In fact, even the most insignificant poetic subject can be remembered with equal value, presented in the same form. Therefore, in their function as records, poetry becomes a contemporary observation of what can be viewed as meritorious; that is encapsulated in the intimate view, and presented by the poet to her audience.

Finally, in writing *Poems to Navigate Caribbean Diaspora Disruptions*, my declared intention is to present subject matters that help to put the experiences, behaviours, histories, memories, politics, religions, culture, and daily life experiences of Caribbean Diaspora migrants into perspective. These poems present illuminating glimpses into their lives, by depicting experiences that embolden them to interrogate everything, in their positions of in-betweenness; between borders, between cultures and between places. Therefore, the Diaspora could also be said to represent a space where multiple identities of people are contested; placed in both the subject and object positions of life, beyond their superficial appearances.

Roselle Thompson
London, 2021

See Glossary
*Roselle & Friends Talk Show

Echoes of Memory

Leave me not, the aroma of boiling hot cocoa-tea and
fried bakes; sizzling roasted cashew nuts and sweet
young corn, spitting friendly on open, wooden fire.
Stay; linger within me, the petrichor of drizzling rain's
pitta-patta, before our tropical torrential downpours.
Let me bask and reminisce in the day's 90 degrees,
sun-drenched, inert air: as it foreshadows the
coming night's twittering crickets and howling dogs.

Remind me of vibrant *kya-kya-kya* bellyful of laughter,
from village girls, being teased by [1]*'force-ripe'* village
boys; with mamaguying catch-phrases like Anancy.
Leave me not, smell of saltfish cooking in black bun-pan.
Let sea-water bathe me once more, with salty healing.
Come to me, the waft of [2]*Limacol* on freshly-washed,
glistening, brown bodies, sprinkled quite generously,
with the soft fragrance of white talcum baby powder.

I implore you to stay, the pious smell of white burning,
soft melted, hot candle-wax; running like pearly tears,
down my naked clenched fist, as I'm gently cajoled
into praying aloud in noisy Baptist-church service;
by mango tree, and Miss Jomen's wooden shack.
Make permanent the distant braying of donkeys,
clucking hens, mixed with querulous feuding voices
of young boys, squabbling over marbles in the dust.

Scorch me again, the peeling hot black tar-roads, that
harden my bare thickened soles, as I quick-march with
purpose; in the persistently streaming, scorching sun.
Hush! I hear the distant [3]*Shango* drums and dream
of dancing with the red-attired women, in tantalising
drunken steps; reviving the nearly-forgotten African
rituals, done deep inside bushes; as bodies and deft
feet move to the long-memorised Motherland beats.

Tell me how these compete with the Islands steel-pan
bands, ancestral [4]*tamboo-bamboo,* and the intrusion
of colonisers' home-grown brass bands; so that my
Memory appreciates with equality, sounds of the
scintillating *reggae* rhythms, infused with [5]*merenge,*
[6]*spouge,* [7]*kaiso,* [8]*cadence,* or [9]*quadrille* twirls; that
cause my mind to sway like a drunkard, in memory's
intoxicating tropical island breeze.

Deep in my diasporic sojourn, I reminisce and peak
at Memory through the window of my soul;
the keeper of minds,
        the bridge-builder,
              between
                      borders,
                            spaces,
                                and
                                      places.

Nos 1–9, see Glossary

Tropical Sunrise Sea

Quietly she lays, gently; as if quivering
Softly in her deep aqua-coloured bed,
Welcoming early cool breezes, as she
Reminisces in wet dreams of long ago.

Earlier darkness has given way to the
Hushed groans of her undercurrent woes,
As she strives with memories of struggles:
Those made to plunge into her depths
Which, for some, seemed a better choice
From painful lives' prison-like travails.

Nightly, she remembers the same dream,
The vivid cries from [1] *Triangle* slave-ships,
And tales of past family-togetherness that
Seemed lost in tireless attempts to let go;
Yet, simultaneously, desperate to remember,
Lest she should forget events 500 years ago.

Now, the silver orb has risen, signalling
Another new day, as his fluorescent rays
Stretch and yawn; whilst summoning heat
Beams to invigorate his spherical charm.
Slowly at first, then stronger, brighter,
He bursts forth behind the horizon's line,
Melting the orangey glow into a silvery hue,
That kisses her shimmering soft face.

Then she rolls over and over, in her
Early morning dance; gently at first, before
Lovingly lap-lapping at edges, helped by
The newly-awakened wind, filled with
The morning's promise of new life, new
Hope, new dawn, and new island-lovers.

She sways and plays, gathering, shimmering,
As she tightens her dark blue dress, aproned
With layers of frothy white [2]*zepingue tremblant*.
Holding her waist tight, she's ready to ride
With crests and dance; enjoying rolls and flips.

Then happily frothing, she turns and froths
Some more, as she begins her horizon journey
To the shore where, she will meet her partners;
The surrounding flora, dressed in green, yellow,
Red, pink, brown, orange, black and blue,
Where they will sway, as they welcome her.

Arriving, she greets them by gently lapping at
The invisible line she's agreed not to cross.
Today, she will delight crowds with kind
Acts of healing, helping, as she caresses the
First-timers, old-timers, the young, the old;
And pleasure-seekers of tropical paradise,
Congregating on miles of enviable sun-soaked
Beaches; laughing, bathing, [3]fêting, and more.

Nos 1, 2 & 3 - See Glossary

The Gift of Flowers

Our earth is the fairest of a thousand galaxies,
Purely blessed with millions of different gifts;
But none is fairer than the rousing opening of
The world's flowers, at the annual birth of spring.
Carefully, deep within her ancient belly, cocooned
Amidst the expansive, thick-brown, light-brown,
Dark-brown, yellowish, blackish-brown soil,
Are Nature's variegated shades – seeds in womb
Carrying latent flowers, that will in time, burst forth,
Undeterred by whatever lies threatening above.

They defy the annual winter burial ceremonies
Of dead trees and plants: but like waiting foetuses,
Gestating in their nine-month, pre-birth stage,
Will drink all of Nature's nourishing nurtients.
Silently, sucking the hidden life-force from her
Soil-bosom deep, they stir and grow imperceptibly.
Yawning, turning and stretching, they are encouraged
By the audible sounds of their Mother's whispering:
Softly, silkily, as under-ground hearts beat in time,
She proclaims the annual pealing of the season's bell.

Above their volatile exterior, men fight against men,
Oblivious of the magical wonders beneath their feet.
But constrained and compliant, like serving soldiers,
Seeds wait for the bugle's call at the dawn of Spring.
Invested with patience they lay in trance-like artifice,
Until their Mother Nature groans, and softly speaks.
Then sounding *The Awake* from her bowel so deep,

These seeds, sweetly, silently waiting and asleep
Push! They stretch, forcing little filigree bodies up;
Upwards, in praise of life towards the heavens.

Push! They breathe softly as their pliable bodies rise,
Awakened by sunlight that kiss their petal cheeks.
And with gentle breezes that hug their slender forms,
They glow; pouring blessings on the waiting land.
In perfect symmetry, they bathe in heavenly tears
That intermittently fall in pre-ordained measure.
Then, perfect in form, and tantalisingly dressed,
They paint our world in millions of myriad colours;
Confirming Nature's delivery of Spring is complete;
As shown by the exquisite bouquets that she gifts.

Words are Bullets

Words
are bullets like
a militant fighter
who pulls his trigger,
then aims it at his foes;
doomed to be maimed
or maybe killed for sure,
as he leaves them to bleed.
Words also can be bullets,
or abstract word-weapons,
when fired at you in tears;
like throwing word-spears,
but without warning shots,
hit hard at your soft heart.
Bullet words can be deadly,
leaves no physical wounds;
they will shatter emotions
then cause bleeding inside.
So if you're tempted to fire
bullet-words in your trigger,
remember, they're deadly -
And cause bleeding for life.

The Old Pub

The spot where the old pub stood;
Is now rubble, rubbish, and broken bricks.
A past social haven for troubled minds,
Where mates met and those who planned
Business got up to some naughty tricks.
A get-away from domestic discontent or
Refuge for the weary after-work; drink,
Steal time, claim solace, forget, reflect,
Remember some of the preceding event,
Or ponder what they may have in store.

The Publican-guvnor's brand of community
Coming together, to drink, talk, argue,
Celebrate, mourn the loss of loved ones;
Or in patriotic fervour watch ambassadors
Of the football game scream at their religion
On giant screens, in this civilised place,
That defies class differences; while, drunk
As a skunk, each man's commitment to their
Team shows fraternity in the pub space.

But that old pub is now a ghost for those
Whose memories recall years of community,
Nurturing and growing stages; now fallen.
So I ponder the resemblance of our own
Buildings that serve us In our youth; maturing,
Mirthful moments, and times of solitude;
Till old age will summon life's demolition

Wrecking-ball, to knock us off our life-perch;
Until we fall, crumble, and disintegrate into
Dust, like the pub now gone; then when absent,
Our lives will become memories of what was.

Natural Woman

She is not defined by labels or your silly slurs,
Or what you think and who you say she was:
She won't be judged by the colour of her skin,
Your media hype or your gender stereotype;
Nor conditioned by your offered token prizes,
But will snub social media *Likes* and its sizes.

Don't dare foolishly orchestrate to berate her,
Your barriers won't keep her down for long;
As relentlessly, she's defiant - mentally sound,
Resilient, unstoppable, and undeniably strong,
So will pick herself up when she's feeling down.

It's not how she chooses to comb her soft hair,
Or the styles of clothes she prefers to wear,
Nor her curved figure that makes you all stare:
She holds chain-reins used to steer her in life,
Loyal, willing, she asks for nothing in return;
But quietly speaks truth, to show her concern.

Despite tasting of life's bitterness and its gall,
She still thrives in the sweet triumphs overall.
Unfettered by grand schemes that threaten
To stain her life, or soften her steely courage,
But will shatter the mind's mental shackles.

Don't try to hide her from the sunlight bright,
Instead, she'll rise like a phoenix bird in flight,
Soaring from ashes to greater heights above;
To present qualities you just can't compare.
She defeats adversity, heartaches, and strife,
To prove she *is* the Mistress of her own life.

Borders & Boundaries

The crossing of borders, boundaries, and barriers,
Has a multitude of very divergent consequences -
From electrocuted wire fences and CCTV defences -
To eyes patrolling divisions and demarcated lines,
Whether imaginary or concrete, will keep you out;
Like penal fences erected to curb your movements,
Instilling fear of incarceration and restriction in cells;
Will hold you back from something that's yours, free -
Breathing air, happily; beyond the envied exit gates.

But innovative expressions of crossing boundaries
Resonate in 21st century epochal break-throughs:
Cloning. Bleaching. AI slaves. Re-assigning genders:
Changes in perspectives once thought sacrilegious.
Today we still cross borders, in order to break free
From internalised boundaries that cause us concern.
Some borders are fiercely defended and will permit
Migration, building of political walls, gender fluidity,
Inter-racial mixes, and globally fused cross-cultures.

And borders set by youths impose limits on movements,
By haunting minds with the terror of marauding gangs
Who secretly threaten to cross post-code boundaries;
To reveal the shocking consequences – a waste of lives
Taken by knife-wielding idiots, who create own systems,
A parallel society with boundaries, codes, secret signs,
Passwords, postal no-go areas, and predatory actions;
To cross man's ultimate barrier, end up in mortuaries -
Frozen in glacial coffins; awaiting boundarised graves.

Education Fail!

She really didn't know that joining the only village
Su-Su Hand was a special African, long-memorised,
Tradition of managing your money; building the whole
Community, tightly knitting families, the local church;
And children who *must* read books, so that a very good
Education will raise theirs and also their people's nose.
After all, it means you've arrived: definitely shows that
Your mind has risen above the 'stupid' ones in the gutter,
So, next you tell yourself you must hurry and compete.

Then brainwashed, you say you can't wait to meet with
All the *educated* ones, who can now explain why being
In the world's foreign spaces, is much better than your
Simple, little, love-filled, wooden, galvanised-roof house;
And your very well-worn, rough, muddy tree-lined yard,
Tiny, tight-knitted villagers, so perfectly Parish-proud,
With the local colourful market town: all, you decide to
Flee from, leaving your lovely, languishing, land behind.

Believing you have to migrate; up, up, and away you fly!
Causing great brain-drain in your *Su-Su Hand* island;
Because now you're *educated*, you have to advance by
Migrating to better lands: beyond your familiar shores.
Until one fine day, rejected in this land, you realise that
A different kind of *education* was needed; so you return!

Su-Su — See Glossary

Elvira's Soul

She died tragically in mysterious circumstances,
Wagged heads, rolled eyes, and knowing glances
Confirmed stories were rife in superstitious tales,
Of doomed pronouncements on all Elvira's males.

Her young life scarred; an illegitimate child she bore,
So she hated and trapped all men she came to know;
She lured them one by one, then she lured them all,
Because her actions had them hopelessly enthralled.

She trapped their hearts with songs as a sweet bird;
Till all the men she knew were infected like a herd.
Ten men she had known and somehow all ten dead
But without proof, really nothing at all could be said.

They say she flew around at night as [1]*La Diablese*,
And many locals wanted her caught, or to confess:
So traps they had laid and cunning vigils hey had set
But with the powers she had gained, avoided the net.

At 21 years escaping from fear, begged for a ride,
Over many, many lands, seeking a place to hide;
Where unknown she would live and try hard to mix,
Among new people, where the past life she would fix.

But soon her evil appetite reappeared once more,
Showed Elvira's wickedness again started to grow:
She hid among the locals in their churches' groups,
Living a pious lifestyle, she even read their *Book*[2]

By day she seemed a kind heart, very willing to give,
At night a vengeful Vampire, sucking blood just to live;
She could rub shoulders with [3]Victor Frankenstein,
Or [4]Jekyll & Hyde, who also did cross their lines.

One day in her sick-bed, she raged and lashed out,
Frightened as Time was closing in, how she did shout!
As her vile soul hastened towards grim purgatory's fire,
She wept, wailed, and whispered one more desire.

To by-pass the hell and horror to many that she gave
Begged for a reprieve, if just one life she could save:
But it was too late; Elvira's soul could never really heal,
So it roams around deciding the fate of lives it seals.

See Glossary
1. La Diablese
2. Victor Frankenstein
3. The Book
4. Jekyll & Hyde

Song of the Caged Bird

Sitting here in limbo,
Preening, pondering,
Watching dramas of strife unfold:
Fathers praying
Mothers crying
Children cursing
Noises drowning
So tired are my delicate ears,
Of this atmosphere of open rage.

So, I sing to drown out their aching sounds,
Knowing it really won't be that long
Before, strangled by their human greed,
They won't be coping; as help they'll need.

Since in their stressfulness,
Distracting forgetfulness,
They will one day say,
Let's throw this flipping cage out today!
Thinking it will solve their perpetual pain;
Throwing me out in the pouring rain.

So, sitting here in limbo,
Preening, pondering,
I'm wishing for little droplets of rain,
And freedom from this life of bane,
As they fight with life's stresses and strain,
Stuck in the *rat race*, the source of their pain.

It's obvious they can't keep up to speed,
With the Jones' who, because of their greed,
Are secretly drug-dealing,
To remain publicly appealing.

So, *my* song is a Blues of
Their brokenness
Their helplessness
Their modern stress
Their foolishness
Which they must one day address.

Sitting here in limbo, I'm singing *their* song,
As I wait to exit this infernal cage of rage!

Migrant Sings the Blues

Happily, I migrated here to live in this foreign land,
Was like a young stallion, when I joined the band
Of courageous migrants, over the Atlantic set sail;
Left all my children, believing this could never fail.

Though risks were great, felt frightened I might die,
Forced parents to surrogate my kids, so I could fly.
Against the cautionary tales of past migrants' woes,
I left all that I knew, to reside on this foreign shore.

My heart's now a frail green trembling callaloo leaf,
Can't afford to eat, so worried I may become a thief,
With anxiety and depression, it's hard to fall asleep,
My nights are long; during which I sit and just weep.

Loneliness is a stranded cat on a big breadfruit tree,
Freedom is not what you make it - just look at me!
Feeling imprisoned, migration's darkened my soul,
I need to go back home, so my life could be whole.

Grand Etang Lake

Like an ancient giant's mirrored mouth,
Eternally opened for Grenada's rainfall,
So is this deeply dark, deceptive liquid;
Expansive, inviting, natural water lake.
Silently she lies; snug, nestled among
The greenest natural forestry reserve.

Grand and motionless, she is ofttimes
Enveloped in rolling masses of mists
That visit early in the tropical morning,
To kiss the nearby evergreen highlands.
Perched 530 metres above sea level,
A hiking trail for ambitious adventurers.

Secretly and slowly, Grand Etang drinks
From local waterfalls and creeks which
Imperceptibly seep into that pure liquid
Imagination; where she's witnessed the
Nation's past history, stories of Grenada,
Civilisation and of conquests; still intact.

Untroubled and unsurpassed by nothing,
She endures the overbearing fiery sun
On its eternal course; it's exhibition is
A shadowless view of the persistently
Blue sky, that reflects on her mirrored
Surface, as it permeates the landscape.

She exemplifies serenity; perfect peace,
In this emerald-green paradise, showing
Off in the vast open air. Like nature's own
Queen of the environment, she is visited
By throngs: but no one knows if, or when,
This extinct crater will ever speak again.

Doh tek yuh eyes an' pass meh!

Leh me carry my God-given frame as ah meant to,
Made like ah shaped from golden brown material
Skin tight, smooth, brown, melanin-shielding being,
Eyes razor-sharp, jewels of my soul's inner woman.

Hair tightly curled cushions acute brain's covering,
With short, medium, long rows, uniquely beautify
My face, adorned by tough ivory teeth that smiles,
And neck holding with pride, the female that's me.

That same body which breathes, lives, procreates,
Have produced several babies from golden brown
Material that expels from womb's racial lineage,
Recognizes me as a queen, with infinite potential.

So doh just tek yuh eyes an' pass meh; no siree!
Ah carry many generations of foreign seed inside,
Like a clay-pot gathering scattered broken pieces,
But still stand dignified, despite bane of slavery.

So doh tek yuh eyes an' pass meh;* no, not at all!
Yuh secretive eugenics enquiry inside our wombs
Doh stopping my advancement; ah forward ever,
Though yuh silent sterility, sodomy, desecrates.

So yuh tek yuh eyes an' pass meh in all yuh films,
Showcasing meh as yuh prostitute, a bitch, a slut,
Or as an uneducated fool, cook, cleaner, a maid.
Perpetuating yuh shameless myths on screens.

As if not enough, yuh sexualise my unique frame,
Yuh really tek yuh eyes an' pass meh; disrespect!
Suggesting it's all ah good for, not yuh queen or
Woman who bleeds, breeds, or needs the same.

And yuh do tek yuh eyes an' pass meh, when yuh
Go straight to white cleaner, thinking he's owner
Of *my* business, or addressing the receptionist
As the boss, when I'm paying her to take *my* calls!

Yes, then yuh tek yuh eyes an' pass meh again,
When yuh questioned my academic credentials,
And refused to believe that my degrees are real;
So stereotyping, yuh spurn my God-given abilities.

But check yuh stupid self, and know that, in truth,
It's meh who's now teking my eyes an' pass yuh;
As ah claim my body to be a Divine temple from
Time immemorial, that's royally made to survive.

So doh tek yuh foolish eyes an' pass meh, no siree!
I'm not receding but increasing; yes, I'm elevating;
Queenly, bronzed, fashioned by fiery experiences
To overcome: so, **NEVER** tek yuh eyes an' pass meh!

Glossary

"Doh tek yuh eyes an pass meh! Means Don't dare disrespect me!
As a Guyanese expression, it's expressed as a rhetorical question
"Yuh tek yuh eyes an pass meh? means, are you trying to
disrespect or belittle me?

I Fell into Heaven

I fell straight into heaven from my bed,
And knocked on ornate golden gates,
They opened with a welcomed mass,
Who happily allowed me to walk past.

'No mourners are here,' voiced my soul,
As a sweet symphony began to unfold;
My thumping heart, was the only drum,
And all senses rose so I felt quite numb.

I hovered among comfy cotton clouds,
That looked as white as heaven's door;
And in the silence and the warmest air
Was pleased to see Him standing near.

A multitude of angels rose; they sang
The merriest tunes with angelic voices;
With harps, bells, and fragrant flutes,
That multiplied extravagances shown.

In this welcoming party of united praise,
I felt the earth received a special Grace
As it strived to make some recompense,
For lost beauty and human decadence.

Accepting mistakes we promised change,
Instantly, it stopped the extinction clock!
I returned from my night of restlessness,
Caused by a dream of such strangeness!

Black Writers

Eagerly they pen their life's experiences,
Ejecting steam within that heals wounds;
Full of optimism, that others will be able
To value their own experiential creativity,
And the holistic consciences of their kind.

But who will really feel as these writers do,
And print their hushed hurts in real books,
For all the world to see; so bare and raw?
Who will judge their distinct dialects fairly,
Without educated understanding, precisely
Where these writers are truly coming from?

The world of past hidden histories hate
To accept outpourings of grief or trauma;
As Ill at ease, with past historic hauntings
They open again; the slowly healing wounds,
Reminding us of uncomfortable subjects
That just don't seem to want to go away.

Imitation, is an adaptive method; a surety
If you can steer away from talking *black*.
Pretence, is an open door of *white* grins
That suck you in; lulling into false security
A belief that the treatment is same for all.

But then, a decade of silent slips of rejection
Shows reality of your misplaced confidence,
In those expected to accept your own words,
Whether they speak of trauma or tribulation,
Ancestral adulation or future pontification.

Truth is, *'privilege'* masks knowledge-lack and
Shows racial experiential qualification needed,
To do justice to your cultural prose, poetically
Assess your words, imagery, ancestral linkages;
Forget that trauma begets traumatic feelings!

A fact lost in a literary world of misapplied
Education: that insists we must stop talking
About racial trauma, as it reveals the cracks,
Of ill-equipped minds wanting to judge the
Literary merit of black trauma-laden lives.

Windrush Betrayal

THEN: *Came the Loud Call*
I wait anxiously, ready to board a migrants' bus from home,
I wait nervously, at the port, speaking in very quiet tone.
I wait quietly, as my passport is checked and luggage too,
I wait patiently, as boarding stewards tell me what to do.

I wait 21 days in Windrush ship: a big British HMS by name!
I wait eagerly, impatient to walk on England's shores of fame,
I wait as arrival taxis came, pick up passengers and then go
I wait vigilantly, whilst witnessing all movements to and fro.

I wait but I'm trembling because the air feels so very cold!
I wait to walk on the British streets that's paved with gold,
I wait and finally it's my turn; late, but my cousin has come;
I wait in hope that he will show me his fancy side of town.

But in the intervening 60 years, slowly, I have grown to learn
That too much work commitment, means I had very little fun,
No longer working, moving towards the twilight of my years,
I'm still **waiting** to deal with some shocking, disturbing fears.

Teresa May's politics say I no longer have my Settled Rights
'Cause Windrush citizens are embroiled in admin oversight;
So anxiously, I wait for sudden sounds that may come near,
Immersed in sinking heart-pangs and real deportation fear.

NOW: *The Silent & Secret Order*
See how it haunts her astonished mind: down-pressed
At the window she stands. Deeply, how it reverberates
In her very soul, as she wonders if she should self-exit,
And end it all; to avoid *Returning* and her ex-pat shame;
With fixed stare, tears; gazes at the sky's drizzling rain.

Motionless: little cries escape from her parched throat
Which quiver like a big leaf; then pulse beats faster,
As coursing blood rages with the hurt and much pain;
So she sobs helplessly, like a child: tear-stained face,
Looking wild, as the suicidal thoughts grip her mind.

But wait - Flashback! History, it's nineteen fifty-nine,
At Southampton harbour: ship docks, carrying British
West Indians with indomitable spirits; valiant subjects,
So confident; were undeniably patriots; and no question
Of wavering allegiance to Britain, had heads held high,
Strong backs to work; they obeyed the Empire's Call.

So Memory walks her through the passage of time,
With elevated recollection and slowly regaining pride,
She fights feelings of doom and sees beyond the *now*,
As slowly, she remembers her past warriors' stance.
So adjusting her self-control, with renewed spirits;
She is triumphantly lifted up on memory's shoulder:
As she decides to live, to tell her own Windrush tale.

THE TALK!
Keeping Black Children Alive

We had such great joy when our little
Beautiful bouncing baby boy was born,
We celebrated with all our friends;
When much pride was lovingly shown.

So, as dear Nick grew up, his yearly
Birthdays all seemed just the same,
As his best friend Simon, whose white
Mother next door, did our party games.

Five years had flown by, and we felt
God in his mercy blessed us for sure,
We teased, romped, played *hide & seek*,
Laughed; Oh my, how you've grown!

We showed you many loving examples
To treat others the same, but by thirteen
Your voice broke, some facial hair-line
Did show, you began to lose confidence.

At school; new fear, caused you to worry,
As unhappily, you were forced to take
Sides among the groups that you knew.
You fretted, worried; didn't want to choose.

And as visits lessened from friends; your
Face reflected what was on your mind,
Constantly showing us a less jolly child,
Our heartaches grew; secretly we wept.
By fourteen, a tall teen, smiling very little,
Your bubbly personality really did change,
So worries stole all our joys; replaced it
With fear of a world with cruelty and dread.

Time for that *TALK*, as heartbeats now skip,
And anxiety grows; our pulse racing, raised
Blood pressure, real rising woes showed,
They grip our lives each day that you wake.

Bidding you goodbye, we look up to heaven
As gesture, in quiet plea for the day's mercy,
And pray as you leave, you'd be back in our
Protected sanctuary; home, where hurts ease.

We send you out in hope, love and in peace,
Looking forward to greeting you with a sigh of
Relief, happy you were spared and returned.
It's not enough living on the edge in such grief,
So we give you a mantra for harnessing peace.

We apologise that we have to give one at all,
But know it may be the difference in avoiding
Black parents nightmare; that most fearful call.
So trying to break the UK's black death-trends;
We offer you this *TALK*; as guidance in defence.

Expect racial stereotypes, despite approaches,
as you're skin-judged; not a biased presumption,
But it's our community's daily reality, that's all.

Your hand dilemma will bring you acute
self-consciousness; so my dear, maintain
their visibility, to be seen, on buses, trains,
on the street; might one day save your life.

Ignore fearful clutching of women handbags
And their quickened footsteps when you're
walking near; beware, these cautions are
to save life; so listen as we show you we care.

We upbraid your dress code; sorry, its
meant to open your eyes wide, of the need
to demystify others' opinion of your racial
dress pride, so we cajole you dress like
the rest, since saving your is the best.

Be aware, fashion styles and colours
though chosen with self-esteem,
could be your undoing: hoodies, doo-rags,
droopy trousers, it seems. So learn to
discern colours that represent the many
kinds of riotously raging wild street-gangs.

Drop friends you think whose actions may
incriminate you in crimes, that's why we
Measure your distance from home and
Your past-time; as being on the wrong
side of the Borough, could cost your life.

*Imposing your time of travelling, is really not
meant to restrict your freedom but to protect
your whereabouts and lessen the panics,
your vulnerability to outside attacks or regrets.
As parent, adviser, teacher, protector, friend;
We have to instruct how to react to the police
when you're stopped: this is advice that you
definitely must always remember to rehearse.*

*And should you feel watched each time
you visit or go inside a shop, know you are
monitored on entry, boldly make all your
actions clear, with steps that are precise
and movements that show you're aware.*

*Operate preferably alone, and my dear insist
on a receipt, even if' it's just for one sweet!
No one should have to undergo such stress or
Strain: bury their child in this world of shame.*

*We know there are long-term consequences;
even with our care, but it's keeping you alive
son, and knowing you will always be near,
We help to navigate the journeys you'll bear.*

*So don't' misunderstand us, but take our advice,
And try to adhere to these solemn suggestions,
without questions, resentment, or even fear;
It's a MANTRA we give you, to preserve your
precious little life: which to us, is very dear.*

Paradise

Oh-ho, so yuh really speakin' English now;
Eh-eh, how come yuh become so Englishified?
And whe' yuh get dis language from, eh?
After yuh so smothered in dem French names,
Like: Grand Ananse, Morne Rouge, Sans Souci,
Petit Balthazar, Ka-fe Beau, Mirabeau,
La Digue, D'Arbeau; even Lance au Epines!
Yuh know dey have Gretna Green in Scotland,
An' Grenville really was a British Prime Minister
Who make sure, yuh cyan forget his colony!

An' how come all yuh Parishes so saintly, eh?
Well yes, yuh right, after all yuh do have a
Paradise; isn't dat near to Dunfermline?
An' ah know also, paradise is paradise -
Yuh know, de ultimate home for godly folks
Like my grandmother an' all de sisters
From de St. Johns Spiritual Baptist church.
Yes utopia, bliss, heaven-bound an' t'ing.
An' in truth, is really so I remember it, eh;
A place dat is real paradise in a child's eyes.

Nowadays, dey say yuh is ah Paradise for
'Tourists, capturing the tropical beauty and
Colours of de Caribbean, with immaculate
landscaping, abundant pools, restaurants,
unequalled resorts, dancing, and feting.'
But isn't it paradise for de globe, since yuh
Spices flavour up de world's food an' drinks?

It's paradise because yuh have our unique
Kick 'em Jenny, active submarine volcano
On Caribbean Sea floor, **an' tropical climate.**

North east trade winds, emerald-green with
Red, gold, an' green, shimmering in yuh flag;
Boastin' nutmeg, symbolisin' sun, people's
Warmth; green vegetation, thrivin' agriculture,
Blended red for harmony, unity, an' courage.
Yes, dat is paradise: place whe' Carib Indians
Spirits smilin' still, because we didn' derive, no!
We were always dere before Columbus' schemes,
Yes, de Creator favour us with paradise status;
So Paradise is what we are, an' will always be.

COVID-19 Directives 2020!

Stay at home and save lives!
Fight, fight against urges rebelling in you,
Defy, stifle and rage against the instincts to disobey.

You *should stay* at home to help save lives,
Because your outing's a virus threat; likely to infect,
So stifle all defiant instincts, urging you to disobey.

You *must stay* at home and save lives,
To prevent the NHS from being overwhelmed;
Defy, stifle and rage against the instincts to disobey.

It's *imperative to stay* at home and save lives,
Please, appreciate your health is our nation's wealth,
So stifle all defiant instincts, urging you to disobey.

Grandad's a passive victim, he is forced to participate,
When you introduced COVID-19, so he expired alone,
You *should have* stifled or raged against instincts to disobey!

Now guilt is your mental shackle: a life sentence you'll battle
That may curse, or haunt you: nothing tears can undo,
For lack of defiance, from urges that overwhelmed, when
You *could have* stifled and raged against instincts to disobey!

Still-birth

Excuse me for dying; I refuse to be born -
In defiance of a life spawned by rape and abject scorn;
From the knocks and the jolts of slave struggle and strife,
Confirms existence that leads to a hellish, harrowing life;
The thorn-filled bed that my mother was forced to make,
Cause rejection of purpose in my life with very strong hate:
From sheer brutality her little life constantly must face,
With no expected upturn my life could possibly embrace.

Excuse me for dying; I refuse to be born -
On Plantation that breeds children just like frog-spawn
Without the love of a sweet mother's proud embrace
Cooing and drooling, soft kisses, with pride of place -
Not a cot, pram, or little blanket for my delicate head,
No one to pass on good news, or happy tears to shed;
No presents, baby showers, or nursery songs I will hear,
But tainted and corrupted lineage is the life that I fear.

Excuse me for dying; I refuse to be born -
Understand my simple logic; please try not to mourn,
No life would be secure, since a slave auctioneer waits
To sell me like cattle, and as the highest Bidder's mate.
He'll ride me like donkey and whip me when drunk,
To cover no self-esteem, as my truth he must debunk
In place of his economic heaven; though his own life is hell:
Understand - this bloody barbarity's no life; even I can tell!

Excuse me for dying; I refuse to be born -
For years I've heard singing, my people *will overcome;*
Surely there's no deity, since all good gods must have flown,
From the few centuries that passed, still no mercy shown;
I waited with patience, wondering what my fate would be,
As I prayed for times with less hurt and a lot less hate:
The slave-masters' own babies are born in love and peace,
I've waited, a [1]mulatto breed; for my acceptance to increase.

Excuse me for dying; I refuse to be born -
With no equality, though we have the same human life-form,
My ancestors were told heaven will reward only if they obey
Slave masters' desires, whose God promises later to repay;
But calling our [2]*Seven Powers*, my people preferred to maim;
Cut limbs, blind eyes, take poison to obliterate the shame,
Of living a life of incessant slave suffering, called on [3]*Legba - God of Crossroads*, to honour our long-held tribal acts of war.

It's now hundreds of years waiting; no change is in sight,
But psychology of scarring and milestones of slaves' shackles
That my people will endure in the coming millennial battles -
Times of subjugation, adopting inferior mindset or feelings;
Since there's no mandate of control, but are left dealing
With a past that still haunts and minds in mental manacles.
As Ancestral Warrior, I must return, so by calling on Legba
To, [4]*'si ilekun fun mi!'* I reject your kind of existence
that denies me freedom to be unshackled on the earth!
That's why I choose dying - I refuse to be born!

Nos. 1 – 4, *see Glossary*

[1]Loki's Return

Boasting forever, he seized fraudulent power,
Spewed venom on laws, as a meteor shower;
Ripped up and cracked all foundation stones
Which for centuries, kept peace in all zones.

Firstly, they laughed at all his brazen cheek,
Secondly, admiring his affrontive gall to speak,
Then normalising destruction, they re-played
His projected emotions, as they were swayed.

Thirdly, fourthly, in dastardly daring degrees,
He forced men to walk on nails on their knees
For failing to adhere to his illegitimate bidding;
Despite seeing danger said, '*He's just kidding.*'

He played them like [2]Orwell's animals on farm,
And many Specialists in numbers did try to warn.
Almost too late, divisions and hate were reeling
From disastrous fate, their '*god*' was sealing.

The battle rages fiercely as history is written,
And many so fearful, in case they are beaten
Became idiotic donkeys who recklessly bray,
Oblivious that democratic zeal is here to stay.

See Glossary
1. Loki
2. Orwell

May their living souls *Remain In Peace* (RIP)

Impacting shock waves, like slamming on brakes,
Of bickering, fighting, and many back-biting make,
When news of death strike with such suddenness,
And says it's time to expose insincerity in sadness.

Breath stop, life left, body cold; now it's very rigid,
A reckoning, reality check, is for the living breed;
Such as Uncle Tom, Aunty Jane, and Cousin Sam,
Who're all engulfed in tempers flaring; tantrums.

Whilst those who did not know her, said they did,
And the same for those faking stories or just hid
Among the living souls, pretended not to quarrel,
All clearing consciences of failure in their morals.

Death came with his evil sister who is called Hate,
But everyone who's penitent said it must be Fate,
That such a young life should so suddenly expire,
When she did not consider or really plan to retire.

Sister Hate brought and spread her vilest venom,
As Uncle Tom and Ben fought over funeral costs,
Sister Pam, and Aunty Jane cried over their lost,
Whilst a funeral feud engulfed like a holocaust.

Then false emotions vied for social media postings,
With comments or *Likes* that need a good roasting;
Surprised, the dead spirit looked on in utter disgust;
At useless words, from those now too late to trust.

Pretending they show empty affections, all very fake,
With lying love-words that conceal the masked hate,
As when alive, these expressions were never shown
So, her spirit now laughing, just prefers to be flown!

Away, to a better place, where it surely doesn't rain,
Sunshine is always bright, with no bickering or pain,
But *R.I.P.* basks in healing music, constantly praying
That the family's living souls, will *remain in peace*.

Motherland Dramas

Roll up! Roll up! Welcome to Empire's fading heartbeat,
Madam! Sir! Come here sit down; please do take a seat.
Here, in land of Royal births and waves it did once rule,
Watch as curtain rises – learn, so you won't be fooled!

The Abbey tolls the knell of the passing Commonwealth,
As prayers said to lament decreasing economic health;
Slave spirits rise, bemoaning silent suffering days of old,
Of centuries' bloodied battles and histories never told.

But from Roman baths settlements and Hadrian's Wall,
Monuments, bridges, fortresses, towers which stand tall,
Castles, cathedrals, and enigmatic Stone Henge's weight,
To Victoria's memorial guarding Buckingham Palace gate.

ALL reflect centuries old histories, of exploiters' conquests,
That scattered migrants like magnets; fallouts from quests.
Now, reversed colonisation in the metropolis' melting pot
Perplexed; some say, 'Too many here, so send back the lot!'

So punctuate your current stories and tell without any fail,
How West Indians were *'claimed'* when Columbus set sail;
He gave Western governments economic warrants as bait,
To legalise their plunders and changed our people's fate.

Now witness the current dramas unfolding in Britain today,
Showing how history haunts us; it's quite karmic they say,
For milk cannot be picked up, once it's already been spilt,
So here we are - evidence of British Empire's past guilt.

Rejection To Influence

Zealously they left with gleeful expectation,
Visualising the golden city from the horizon.
Planned how to excavate reported treasure,
Whilst Windrush sailed the mighty oceans;
No one thought of the awaited rejections.

Saturated in their English colonial religion,
Prayed God will spare them from attrition,
Since expectation of religious-globalisation,
Almost at their grasp, hope was that it lasts
Fretted; reached Southampton Dock at last.

Believing, these braves took on the mantle
With fervour, as they tried to finally settle.
Hearts white as snow, Sunday they'll show
How Jesus loves them, equally they know;
Until doors slammed, words cut like blows.

Resilience grew strong, black skin grew thick,
They started their own, and sparsely mixed,
Began churches at home, their roots did show
Worship was easy in the ways they all know;
No more sitting quietly, while spirits groaned.

Then filling their souls, cried loud *Hallelujahs!*
Clapping, singing, complaints were popular;
Shouting, dancing, as protests grew stronger,
So community centres, halls, worship spaces,
Accommodated our people's church places.

As UK Christian landscapes began to change,
The British Christian Scholars did rearrange
The labels for this wonderful phenomenon;
Regretted allowing Black churches formation,
Struggle greatly to fit them in regimentation.

Pondering over their thirst for labelling said,
We wondered, should we just call it black-led,
Black majority, minority ethnic, or Windrush
Churches, even Caribbean Pentecostal as such?
But noted our independence without any fuss.

Whilst their Christian fortunes began to decline,
Black churches helped in their come-back climb,
Rescued Britain from doom of laxed secularity.
With percentage rises in Boroughs across cities,
Now they laud over Black churches' activities.

Rich Man, Poor Man, Beggar man, Thief!

Often, foolishly taken for granted, is wisdom's simplicity,
When *Intelligent* men are blinded; oblivious of its reality,
Prefer to overlook its frank honesty and plain philosophy.
So, who's to blame for circumventing Solomonic solution?

Rich man, poor man, beggar man or just a plain thief!
Difference is hidden by ignorance; it's also a wise belief;
Living categorised, prioritised, boundarised; we all must
End up levelled in simple oneness; an equality that is just!

So, give a man greater height than the lowly poor fellow,
Indulge him with all the trappings of life - pretty shallow,
And myths of perfection or elevation, privilege, and such,
Tell the world he is one who should not at all be touched.

Surround him by fortress, with ferocious forces that tear
Your flesh up, for debunking their silly folly over the years
And saying it's unjust; they baulk at your sole resistance
In failing to bray like the rest: disliked for your defiance.

We breathe the same air, feel weak, at times we get sick?
Or was the pain you felt, a rich one: different, more chique?
Do you bleed the same red or is mine tinged with less hue?
Or your skeleton wealthier than a beggar in his rotten shoe?

Do tell me that your organs shape and function as the poor -
Same for the rich man, poor man, beggar man, and the thief!
In death, all hearts stop beating; as spirits return to the sky,
'Cos riches can't buy immortality from the Master on high.

So unchanged, all dead bodies must return - *dust-to-dust*,
Where worms mocking, laugh at our silly categorising lust,
Since we're interred, in the same, simple, unclassified earth,
Awaiting the rich man, poor man, beggar-man, and the thief!

Soucouyant Bite Me!

Shooting red flames in tropical sky at night,
Village people in folktales, have her in sight,
Shedding her skin, she hides it in a big tree,
Skinless – she's looks for children with glee.
Mistress of the moon and skies
Village people are also very wise.

They hear her shrieking, mournful cries,
Squeezing in the door cracks, she rises,
She prowls in baby's room as he sleeps,
Closer she moves, for his blood to seep.
Mistress of the moon and skies,
Village people are also very wise.

She made her pact with Basil the devil,
Trading blood for his powers that's evil,
But must return before morning comes.
Or salty, peppered skin will forever burn.
Mistress of the moon and skies,
Village people are also very wise.

They saw her leave then took her skin,
Rubbed salt and pepper to pay for her sin;
When the baby cried, a boy and a girl too,
'Soucouyant* bite me!' So everyone knew.
Mistress of the moon and skies,
Village people are also very wise.

Then high across dark black sky she did shoot,
A flaming red streak of light, the form she took,
Then searched for her skin inside the big tree;
"Oh skin, it's me, you nah know? Skin, it's me!"
Mistress of the moon and skies,
Village people are also very wise.

She has no skin, now that her cover is blown,
Her identity public, all deceit will be known,
A blood-sucking Soucouyant caught in daylight,
So her future is not really looking too bright:
The wise and cunning old villagers did say,
'We are the people; will catch you one day!'

*Soucouyant – see Glossary

Ciara's Costly Catastrophe

A storm will hit England? No, not us — it's unbelievable and far-fetched.
A real storm, surely someone must have got it wrong, so some did bet!
As repeated news irritation, an unusual storm coming this time of year,
Broadcast dismal News faces in transmitted warnings showing fear,
Charts display how it would strike us hard; as amber warnings showed
That England would be besieged, lasting attacks - so stay off the roads.

But how some had jeered at the impossible idea, saying there's no need
To worry about the storm's severity or its predicted strong wind speeds,
And the accompanying gales that will bring us forceful lashings of rain:
So the newsfeeds of flooding met with derision, were expressed in vain,
For those not heeding warnings, regardless of cautionary story boards,
Were surprised at Ciara's stealthy entry with artistry, when she roared.

She assaulted the tall trees, so they bowed, swayed, riotously waved,
Then nervously danced, trembled, twisted low and some even cracked.
Ciara increased her invisible force with strong and powerful demands,
Began to wail in crevices, squeaking, hissing loudly in all cracks,
So omnipotently the heavens opened its windows and boldly sent forth,
Torrents flowing in surges; creating instant, roadside lakes in bends.

As if a hand opened taps, water pounded on England's surfaces in sight,
Like the Baltic's bitter billowing waves, water filled up all paths.
Casualties were noisy; bins flew so wild, as many roof tiles broke loose,
Eyes stared in disbelief behind rain-smeared windows, safely indoors
Watching; as nature's fearful symmetry turned from a calm, sunny day,
To raging, wintery, anger; like a tiger lashing out in painful defence.

She turned streets into a scary, ghostly paradise, as many ran quickly,
Desperate to salute homes in awkwardly uttered words of gratitude,
Lucky they had made it inside; where they would try to comprehend
How such a storm could hit England, and precisely as had been foretold.
Now they face consequences of homes mired in muddy, slushy terrain,
Where cars and people floated as debris in rising, temporal tide;
Evidence of Ciara's visit; a costly, catastrophic, climaxing conclusion.

Storm Ciara - See Glossary

Ode to the Sun

Good morning, all hail to the sun!
Sphere of a million tiny golden stars,
Turning our dark nights into days,
After you chased the murky ghosts
That lurked in the shadowy nights,
Away from our comfy little house.

Hail the sun! The hottest star, giving
Us light, and life-infused uniqueness,
With brightness of love and pure joy.
You make all our glad hearts heave
With your honey-filled, sun-tastes,
Of hot yellowy, mellowy, loveliness.

So our days await your encircling,
Of soft, sun-shiny, silky, snug kisses
As you bathe us with incandescence,
Feeding our spirits with light and life,
And promises of real commitments
To beauty and hope; love and peace.

Oh golden orb of nature wrought!
Distilling fears within our thoughts
Rising. Setting. Unfaltering on your
Axis: picture-perfect and so precise;
Regulating all our days' movements,
Then says *good morning* once more.

The Broken Clay Pot

Their lives are now broken pieces of the clay pot;
Splinters, deep layers from the rich, brown earth,
The original, intact; invested with a perfect form,
Like an innocent urn; pregnant with possibilities.

Forged from the fiery furnace of pure beginnings,
Its role was to instil pride and impart knowledge;
To nation-build a future heritage for the children,
A prototype for birthing nations of astute minds.

Its overriding mission, to ensure those offspring
Produce centuries of philosophers and scholars;
Scientists who could travel to the moon or mars,
But they were displaced; children of the clay pot.

The brokenness curtailed their natural creativity
To be innovators who discover unique formulas
For the common cold; and the capacity to invent
A cure for cancer's tenacious grip on all mankind.

Matriarch of millions, mourning scattered pieces
From your soil of civilisation; priceless, they exist
Like rocks, uniquely imbuing the skills of survival,
Yet are malleable to manoeuvre from shrinkage.

Despite dispersal, see how they cling to vestiges -
Qualities from the original clay pot, which persist
With challenges; whilst waiting for reconnection;
Inevitable reclamation of your scattered pieces.

A Bright Shining Star!

Strange, how the capacity to rule dominions is ofttimes feared,
By those who see a bright shining star and treat it with dread;
Like rubbishing your sweet poems, banishing your astute brain,
For fear it could stitch them in zigzag words, or twisted thread,
Like embroidered knotted patterns, covering your bed-spread.

They may even put you in a closet and throw away the only key,
Or perhaps peeping, look to see if you can breathe, eat, even see!
How pugnacious are the empty minds of those whose only goal
Is to steal all your joy, and hope that it will cause you great pain,
In exchange for their secrets; as your rebellion cries out in vain!

Trying to out-manoeuvre them, you criss-cross stitches over lives,
Till poisoned by their lies, their knotted lives scream *Let her live!*
Because guilt wreaks havoc in their haunted minds, threatening
To reveal conspiracies that tarnished and caused a great shame;
So disturbed by their pilfered fame, they confessed your name.

Surprised that you survived the storm, and no longer repressed;
You observe how their waning lives are now worm-eating flesh,
That begins to die in your poems: a weapon that cauterizes lives,
Like serrated knives; your words as deep wounds, bleed inside;
Now your dominion's returned, it hastens their parallel demise.

The Enemy Within
(A poem of Hope in 2020, during COVID-19 Pandemic)

The empty streets speak to a ghostly existence,
As the enemy creeps silently stalking us to blast,
Threatening our strong sense of safety defences,
While Death reigns omnipotent and we feel aghast.

It strikes at loved ones, our enemies, and friends,
Especially our vulnerable elderly - its preference;
This onslaught of disease makes us all ill at ease,
As the silent plague rages seeking whom to seize.

The invisible bombardment began infiltrating slow,
Threatening our healthcare systems, aims to show
Collapse; whilst lack of basic supplies did multiply,
Reveals our unpreparedness; nonetheless, we try.

No time for big titles, no time for class difference,
But scenes of politicized chaos display irreverence.
It equalises age, gender, colour, religious sections,
As every ideological faction hit with this infection.

Mocked by the rats who now raid in our absence
And joined by foxes rummaging in silent city fence,
We sit inside homes in *Lock-down* for our defence,
As past revelling echoes with a distant eerie sense.

Police will march as extra capacity to overthrow,
As we stand together to oust this murderous foe;
As Fear stokes hospital corridors with much dread,
Bodies clog up beds and sadly a lot are now dead.

Expecting the wounded and fallen along the way,
The battle raged on as frontline medical staff sway -
But hit hard by the virus' vicious spitfire-like attacks,
We applauded them while defiantly they fight back.

So tell pupils, who enjoyed their time off school,
We all came together to serve soup as we should,
Caring for the homeless, prioritising the very poor,
Until UK conquers COVID-19; or boot it out the door!

Wedding Picture

They say a picture can tell us a lot in a thousand words,
So why, oh why, had this one only stopped at just 999?
Wasn't their picture full of present love and promises -
Of blissful satisfaction for all future hopes and dreams?

There it sits in golden frame, dominating the main room;
Gigantic - the laughter it shows are genuine from groom;
Look at him, proud and passionate, a cricket-loving youth,
Smiling sweetly, as he gently embraces his young bride!

Royally, his Sherwani suit, perfect in embroidered art silk,
Matches his turban with precious golden embellishments,
Studded into the material, that exudes a rare regal aura:
It extols beauty, brightness, wonder, love to please her.

His full-length, white tunic is truly unsurpassed by none.
A Maharaja. Majestic. Confident. Accompanied by his
Very bejewelled bride, emblazoned in a bright red sari,
And generous gold trimmings that cling to slim figure.

Underneath this, her young slender body birthed sweat
Surreptitiously, through a heavily made-up baby face,
As she endured feeling suffocated by doting females -
Those who obediently observe their traditional norms.

So every eye movement was followed without dissent;
Fussing ¹*Ammas,* ²*Appas,* ³*Chitthappas,* ⁴*Periyappas* more;
Well-wishers, friends, and photographers blinded them,
As cameras competed to capture their innocent dawn.

Mountains of various wedding gifts gave encouragement,
Whilst their business and own house boosted confidence;
They planned a family with all schools located nearby,
Therefore only a fortuitous future of bliss should multiply.

But no one had imagined that all would soon be marred
News of a virulent brain tumour, so sudden; death's hard!
But he left his precious cricket bat; memorial for the kids,
Who chose cricket, believing he would have been pleased.

Glossary

1. **Tamil** for Mothers, ²Fathers, ³Mother's sister husband, ⁴Fathers brother

The World is not enough!

The world is not enough for those who,
Contemptuous of our generations past,
And disregarding their sacrificial deeds,
Would menacingly, tread precariously;
Spurning laws and stoking discontent.

For many modern leaders breaking rules,
Provide the persistent punitive examples
Of thoughtless, deep-rooted, putrid hate;
Which suggests the legacy of our fate is
Inevitable: a festering, purulent volcano.

Pregnant with weaponry of destruction
Men convert feeble minds to strike first,
At those now buried in their city's rubble,
Then try to convince us the action is just:
Only secures a surety, revenge is a must.

But some take a stand in the torrid path,
Like conscientious objectors; won't kill
The truth: a word once revered by aged
Philosophers, those with great capacity;
Scholars of integrity and magnanimity.

They have fought the monstrous media
That stokes competitions of nuclear feats;
And stir in dark hearts and boastful minds
To strike. Kill. Then, as invisible as the air,
All fall dead; spurning our only civilisation.

Perplexing to those who are still trying to
Find answers to the real meaning of life;
We all succumb to the annihilating truth,
That Nature's innocence perhaps is lost,
In a world that seems no longer enough!

Our Village

There it is, **ONCE** home, our land; happy, we did care,
Little material wealth but love we had for all to share,
Cooking on woodfires, blowing smoke makes you cry,
Make soup, bakes, plantains, fritters, wet fish to fry.

There it is, **ONCE** dark nights, frogs near roads with ruts,
Vehicle, no street light, snakes hide in the wooden huts:
Working on land: cut grass, pick mango, drink cocoa tea,
Wash clothes in river, climb trees, hills: bathe in the sea.

There it is, **ONCE** filled with crowing cocks, pigs, and goats,
Waiting for scarce transport, walking miles on hot roads,
Heavy loads on [1]*kata*, balanced on top head, neck carry
Bananas, fruit, fire-wood, water in pan: never in a hurry.

There it is, **ONCE** witness chattering children and old folks,
Walking outside, greeting, scolding kids; or telling jokes;
[2]*Liming*, drinking, cursing, teasing, laughing; debating men,
Singing, cooking, plaiting hair; caring from pretty women.

NOW there are changes: the community is too busy to care,
Plenty material wealth, money, and foreign food to spare:
Rejection of what's homegrown, with no time to share,
Transport so speedy, it races and glides, as if in the air.

NOW men are busy; no time to debate, chat, laugh, or [3]*lime*,
The inside washing machine replaced rivers; it cuts time,
Home-produced goods re-sold, re-packaged, you buy,
Conceal in Ex-pats' fairy-tale mansions; tall as the sky.

NOW perched dangerously on hilltops, they now compete,
Blinding electricity, to block [4] *ole-time* story-telling feat.
Tourists seeking home-cooked cuisine and our culture too,
Find it's not available, but KFC and McD; these will now do.

NOW dark Coca cola flows like witches conjuring brew;
See how things are overthrown; it's time that you knew,
Time to open your mind, with concern, you must share,
Talk of threats to our culture - act now - if you dare!

Glossary
1. *kata* - a roll of cloth or vegetation placed on top of the head to cushion the skull from the weight of a head load.
2/3. *liming/lime* - meaning to hang out or chill with friends
4. *ole-time* – something done a very long time ago e.g. tradition or custom

A Voice Our Own!

Strophe I
Isn't it patently obvious that
Forcefully wrenched from the
Cradle of Civilisation's Comfort,
Greedy ravaging exploiters
Had a plan to plunder lands
With no calculation of an end?
But all roads to colonisation,
Led to a slave trading Triangle
With a tunnel vision to force,
Rape, pillage, prey and poach
Humans from their own peace.

Strophe II
Using vulgar terrorism or dread,
Destruction and degradation,
And the vileness of castration
Of men, he elevated himself –
Coloniser. Master. Thief!
Brutally, he choked the lives
Out of those he overpowered,
But claimed his own soul was
Religiously, heaven-bound!
Manipulated his dark minions
To tremble at his colonising
Language and mis-education,
Division and desperation.
Greed. All-white coveting
In reality, postulated theft -

Of all our culture's wealth -
The mark of his Slave Trade.

Strophe III
The bitter sea journeys were
Graves for the fortunate few -
Tossed overboard, dead human
Cargo who limbo-danced to whip!
Crack! Cries! Wail! Woebegone!
Created life-times of divisions,
Dispersal, existential blindness,
Deceit, subjugation, wickedness!
Lives forced to do obeisance
To inhumane acts from madmen,
Were denied their basic Human
Rights - freedom, family, friends.
Supremacy - his divisive weapon,
In claiming Divine Right to commit
The world's worst act of atrocity.
His blatant bombastic arrogance
Led to some underground defiance,
As strong will and Anancy-cunning
Cause overthrow with rebellion,
Conspiracy, wisdom, slave fraternity.

Strophe IV
Now the synthesis of cultures
Springing from ancestral dualities
Leave imprint of fragmentation -
Multiple bloodied backgrounds of
Interrupted lives tainted by colonial

Powers, assassins' misdemeanours,
Cause kaleidoscopes of backgrounds.
They carry deep, post-colonial, wounds,
Linguistic variations and identity quests
That lead to radical searches for roots
Amidst the growth of Black aesthetics,
Rising consciousness and Black power.

Strophe V
Artistic intentions to check out and
Re-create an identity and language
Of their own, grew with impatience,
Via declared intentions for society's
Redirection. Recreation. Restoration.
They took a stand to re-write their
Own version of events - from tribal
Purity to blemished mixed pidgins,
And Creole vernaculars or vestiges
Of European-based cultural varieties,
Accumulated as we birthed our own
Language, unique [1]*Nation Language*.

Strophe VI
So accentuating a radical shift to
Deliberately rise in consciousness,
We turn the tables and sing, we speak,
Talk, dance, act, and instruct, to
To *tell it like it is* to the masses,
In our epoch of post-colonialism.
Strategically, recapturing African
Spirituality, we fly our flags of
Homegrown integrity and pride.

Strophe VII

Despite the global migrating trends
Forcing a multitude of other inputs,
We highlight relationships of *continuum*
Reflecting emergence of our oral-scribal,
Audio-visual, musico-dramatic, voice in
Performance-based Creole; our artistic genres.
So now you know before multiculturalism
And transnationalism and global integration,
There was me, pluralistically made, to reflect
Fusions of oral and linguistic backgrounds
That makes our unique [2]*Caribbean Orature!*
The identified Voice and Variety of our own!

See Glossary
1. Nation Language
2. Caribbean Orature

Trauma Begets Trauma

If only he'd known that the pain and indelible trauma
of the beatings he gives her, started long ago from capture;
CRACK! WHIP! CRACK!

That same pain became pregnant, with need to reproduce
On slave ships, carrying chained people, for monetary gain;
WHIP! SKIP! LIMBO! CRACK!

Multiplied daily in the plantation estates to work harder;
WHIP! WORK! WHA-DAP! WHIP! WHO-EE!

Brought forth offspring following brutal raping with force;
IN SOUNDS TOO PAINFUL TO NAME!

Grew children who knew the same trauma, too young;
WHIP! RAPE! MAMA! HELP ME!

ALL cries seem to reverberate an eternity, with ghosts in the wind;
CRACK! WHIP! SKIP! WHA-DAP! WHO-EE! RAPE! MAMA! HELP ME!
AND SOUNDS TOO PAINFUL TO NAME.

So deeply, indelibly ingrained In generations of all our people's psyche,
Infused in each victim's blood, he persistently emulates the same shame;
By beating his woman with his fist, then a stick - all come with his 'love.'
It's what he knows, a sign to tell others he's '*maste*ful,' the way he cares;
So she beats their children, whom she loves, as education to remind them

To beat their children: as a way of showing that you love them, with licks.
So they will become women and men who must also beat each other up
From home to the street, in ways that show *mastery* over someone's life.

But the children have swapped the fist and the stick, for a gun and a knife,
With experiences showing how easy, to take another child's precious life.
And families have no qualms conspiring lies, to wreck, raid, and ruin, their
Unsuspecting auntie's successful life: it hinders the master's stereotypes.
So plan with co-conspirators, take Judas' price, to perpetuate their myths,
That those from your heritage are worthless, as the violence shown on TV.

It backs up their records of criminality, reinforcing trauma of racial divide.
Remember, that same pain is indelible trauma; it just keeps on repeating;
over the years, decades, and centuries, until one day, you **MUST LEARN** to:

STOP the gun and the knife causing deadly pains,
STOP the big stick from automatically lashing out,
STOP a husband's angry fist from pounding his wife,
So she can **STOP** herself from flogging their children,
Till each one, teach one, how to **STOP** and question
The source of their pain, and their reasons for actions,
That comes from repeatedly memorised, painful hurts; long ago.
So healing must flow from concern and conscious awakenings,
Till reparation teach us to observe the results of recurrence.
We say **NO** to the continuous lineage of our harmful hurts,
And cycles of centuries-old damage to the psyche; in order to
Reverse patterns of deeply ingrained, imitative, unconscious, trauma!

I am Somebody Great!

Say it, *'I am Somebody Great!'*
Say it; it will change your fate;
That's what she always said,
Say it, aloud before going to bed.

So we tried it and surprisingly,
It showed that something *great*
Did happen to those who needed
To rise from their 'bottomless pit.'

This nugget birthed many qualities
That seemed to have been buried
Deeply; it invigorated the helpless,
And gave hopefulness to the poor.

It motivated so-called 'uneducable'
To aim high; to reach for the sky,
And like magical golden chrysalis,
They did achieve successful wings.

Proving that once stirred within
Mentally, its belief cannot reverse.
The achievement of *somebody great,*
Is a testimony of life that's renewed.

Once it's born, cannot be returned
To the place where it once was,
But as a phoenix in flight it soars,
Ensuring you remain a *Great Somebody*.

I Saw a Ghost

I saw a ghost once; ten feet tall,
Standing near our kitchen wall,
Dressed in tribal attire so bright,
He looked a sad and sorry sight.

His eyes, two vacant Gobi shells
Did stare like evil bats from hell,
Glaring in pitiful and cold silence,
His face was a ghostly transience.

No clothes were upon his back;
He poured out oil from a big sack,
Then chanting a very familiar tune,
Pointed at the night's big moon.

He beckoned me to join and sing,
Whilst offering me a pretty ring;
Then floated on like fluffy clouds
With laughter that was very loud.

No shoes or socks upon his feet
But he danced to a familiar beat;
His steps and rhythm did unite,
I marvelled at this strange sight.

In tongues I knew not how I spoke,
I softly sneered at his hidden yoke,
And in the voice of an angry Sage
I denounced his deceit with rage!

Diversity's Dilemma

It's called diversity; because diverse people share the city -
London: But men and women, viewed with cultural dread,
Each clamour for a slice of the long-dead Empire's bread.
Unknowingly, reversing colonial trends; and like Anancy,
Are adding to society's fabric, their own patch of ubiquity.

Like neighbours on stage they pretend to pace the boards,
With grinning masks on, exchange discriminating glances
On wild, winter days; and cold, cloudy, crispy, autumns,
Await spring, which will control the waxing and waning
Of the soft, sunshine days and swirling summer breezes.

As seasonal diversity does obeisance to perpetual cycles
Of nature's lead, humans mimicking her simple supremacy,
Often boast of annual *'black'* months of *'history'*-easing
Consciences; which imperceptibly, reveal national bigotry,
That taints young, defiant, minds with angry questions.

Lifting sordid lids off hidden pots of past atrocities done
In the empirical expansion, it resurrects hearts of wounds
Around inner city lanes; where frightful gang-led terrains
Resemble patchwork quilts of diverse cultural infusions,
And festering oases of intolerance from repressive living.

Simultaneously, men and women in suburbia witnessing
Differences, hide among high-gated, high-class quarters,
Will bemoan diversity's folly, and blame ruin of their city
On immigrants; regret they welcomed the idea of variety,
Will forget the nation's need of foreigners' productivity.

Then vote for one-culture, white privilege, or preference,
Will starve, as restaurateurs and staff return 'back-home,'
And hospitals' care collide; collapse without staffing levels
That cared for the sick, saved the dying; despite the abuses,
Ensured longevity, and protected the qualities of our food.

How diverse will be the regrets as they rue their visionless
Minds' short-sightedness, or crass, quick-tempered tongues!
Then, various rejections will measure the diverse reactions;
From broken, divided families, to the loss of familiar faces -
All lamenting replaced void and multiformity's brokenness.

Go on, Laugh!

Go on, laugh! Laugh in your unrestricted bubble of happiness,
Protected by your pure innocence and sunlight from within.
Laugh; by laughing you celebrate life, your Divine right to do;
Free from the worries, the cares, and concerns of our world.
Let your laughter ring in our ears, as a balm for our woes.

Laugh at virus threats, to obliterate guardians in your space,
Whilst loved ones insist you soar above the mess with grace.
Laugh, and enjoy life in your bubble of unbridled happiness,
Play *hide-and-seek, skip, catch-ya* – for as long as you can,
It's your rage against COVID-19 which wants to spoil your fun.

Laugh, as protectors fight to ensure you'll be laughing long,
To forever fill the air, as it resonates in your playgrounds,
Cleverly hushed in corridors, laughter becomes whispers,
Where grinning wide, your confident glances assure us that
You've inspired the little shy fearful ones in seats near you.

So laugh, sing, write, read, and learn; as you know next day
You'll be back to laugh some more; carefree, unrestrained,
You'll march to the morning's school gate, anxiously rush in
And laugh; you repeat the daily cycle, oblivious of dangers -
The pandemic storm that's raging around your school door.

Yours is the future, so laugh, study, and learn to discern
From play, and strength, how to rid the world of COVID ills,
Public disquiet, confusion, and terror; as it multiplies pain.
I know your persistent laughter is your own way of raging
Against all threats to curtail your little lives at this stage:
So, go on laugh, and enjoy the bubbles of your happiness.

Reality Hits Home!

It's pandemic time, no choice, prohibited; can't share,
Though we really would like to show you that we care,
Can't fly back, give, even send; don't know what to say,
No work, or real play, but must stay indoors - all day!

Remittances home plunged, hungry bellies are on fire,
We watched TV news, as the virus rates rose higher;
While the solemn guidelines read like war-time news,
And theories-filled minds checked the Facebook views.

Banks incomes in countries, plummeted causing fright,
Endured worst remittance decline; such a terrible sight!
But beaches stayed clean, as dumped plastics lessened,
And air rejoiced from less pollution; oh, such a blessing!

Animals roamed freely, so glad for the extra territory,
As the gun and knife crime rates decreased in our city,
Screens all aglow; heaven forbid, if internets crashed,
Or disturb life-lines for kids' worlds; curtailed in a rush.

Perhaps the local shopkeeper cried quietly in his bed,
Regretting times he treated his customers with dread!
Weekly, flinching as bank balances mocked his decline,
Cringed daily as shoppers bought their goods online.

No physical embrace, to quell distant lovers heartaches,
Whilst cheating pairs, nothing going on, just had to fake,
And money-grabbing religions, with no big Sunday tithes,
Appreciated all their members, as Zoom services sufficed.

But I counted all the time saved, minimal cost on my expenses,
And realised the restrictions reinforced more of the positives;
Of not how much I had lost during times of COVID lock-downs,
But really how much I had gained, putting away all my frowns:
Now I laugh, as my glass is not half-empty; instead it's half-full.

The Fear Of Returning

After 60 years of bracing England's cold,
Still they dream of returning home one day,
To the paradise they carry inside of them,
Whilst working to buy a big piece of land,
To build a mansion outside of the village.

Forgoing all types of leisurely activities;
They pretend summer breaks do not exist,
As they anticipate, dream, and visualise,
That one day, not-too-distant in the future,
They will be returning to their 'back-home.'

Working day in, day out; come rain or shine,
Summer, autumn, or winter, and spring,
Many years roll back; then ageing, mature,
Bodies slow down, and energy dissipates,
As skeletons degenerate causing sickness,
But returning is still a clear vision in sight.

Bodies weak, though minds are very intact,
Planning, they listen to the *back-home* news,
Punctuated with spiralling rates of crimes,
Increased economic hardship, and insecurity
Shake them to the core; question the safety
Of returning for good or choose to remain.

Tethered to their *homes*, they keep social ties,
But who will heal their new diasporic traumas,
Of fearful reintegration to their nation fabrics,
And the reality of culturally diluted lifestyles,
Or stomachs intolerant to *ground provisions?

Who will guarantee their safety, from those
With criminal intent, desperate to prey with
False notions, all about wealthy expatriates;
Reversing El Dorado myth: that they brought
Tons of wealth from England's golden streets.

Worse, are those who think returnees will
Readily invest in large-scale developments,
And projects of charitable causes, as they
Live and conduct businesses in their island:
Showcasing their foreign inter-dependence,
Foreign attitudes, foreign clothes and speech.

But who has thought of their ageing needs?
The poverty-stricken, sick; making last-ditch
Attempts, to claim Caribbean space again;
Some illegally dumped in fake deportation,
Penniless, homeless, family-less, shamed;
Wait for the Master's last knock on doors.

Needing health care, or medical support,
Social services, and recreational activities,
Who will fund them in their ageing years,
Or create the age-appropriate living space,
With specialised services for their needs?

Pondering their reality, they go back and forth
On limited time, to keep their entitled benefits.
Hoping, they admire the waiting piece of land,
With fairy-tale house cocked-up on top big hills;
All which become their current life challenges.

Caught in a dilemma of being between borders,
Heavy hearts, woebegone, they plane-commute,
Capitulate to familiar racism, dehumanization;
Until exiled bodies are laid to rest; since they
Did not visualise a *return* home in weakness.

Glossary

***Ground provisions** is the term used in Caribbean islands to describe a number of traditional root vegetable staples; such as yams, sweet potatoes, dasheen root (taro), eddos and cassava. Thy are called ground provisions because they grow underground. They are also locally called *biandas, food, grung provision, hard food, and ital food.*

When the words just won't come!

Just one word, anything please - to begin!
Just one; any little, relevant, word to strike.
Oh, where's the missing Muse of Creativity?
And for how long will She really be gone?

Sighing noisily, taking long hissing breaths
That spell *B-L-A-N-K F-R-U-S-T-R-A-T-I-O-N*,
I try to write but doodle comes out instead,
Making curly scrawly lines on my blank page.

Then strange lines begin to form letters,
As Creativity powers pen to make shapes
Into words, and then, a whole line - comma,
As she breathes her new life into my page.

Now awaken, we both breathe in unison,
Our spirits intertwined; ideas come flowing
Lovingly, as we give birth to words with life
And meaning on the page; no longer blank.

So, I welcome back my sweet Creativity!
Heart and soul of inspirational intimacy.

'Death' Does Not Become Her!

Her summer sun did rise up at dawn,
And on media show-case it was born,
From morning to noon and also at night,
Her determination, to do what's right.

Papers print their bold and brazen lies,
Seeking ignorant minds, or foolish eyes,
Happy to poison whilst they fabricate,
Gain sensations, causing needless hate.

Her fear was real, her heart felt hurt,
Like jelly, life became an unsteady rut,
She raged inside, feeling so very alone,
As Editors cursed her life; with scorn.

She smiled a lot and smiled some more,
With stiff upper lip, grinned, as she bore
The criticisms, while more lies were told;
Feeding readers, who just wanted more.

Delighted with newsflash, pictorial rage,
Media scorned her on their front pages;
Her pain festered could no longer fight,
As public show trial was surely in sight.

The news media became her daily dread,
She couldn't control the pain in her head;
Skies were grey, when her job was lost,
Instead, inside courts her life was tossed.

Cooped up like an animal inside her home,
As fair-weathered friends all clearly flown;
Couldn't comprehend the life that's shown,
Stared from her windows feeling all alone.

Mind flashed back to former glorious days,
When laughter echoed, lovely as sun-rays;
Her future looked good; so awfully bright,
Everyone agreed she was a beautiful sight.

But dying eyes mirrored the fake laughter,
She blocked, concealed all pain inside her;
Vowing to soldier on, in spite of all the bile,
Obscured warning signs behind all smiles.

Did she envisaged death to overcome fears -
Deaden constant gut-pangs and all tears?
Inquisitors persistently pursuing in waves,
Clearly, paving the way for her early grave.

When her mind plunged into a dark abyss,
No one was around to protect her life's bliss
Or see chains that constricted her little life
As she toyed with ending it all with a knife.

We seek in life art of finding perfect peace;
Hers shattered: in fact, savagely decreased
On D-Day: so with deep and deadly decision,
They won a conspiracy but failed the mission.

Just Come!

Come to me though weary and weak,
Laden, beaten or broken; just come.
Come with your heart full of the hurts
That life has besmirched; just come!

Come to me, look, see; I'm beckoning
To show you how to forget the pain,
And take off the stress or heavy strain,
To fight off life's cold rain; just come!

Come to me, taking one step at a time,
Holding lowly head high but with pride;
We'll navigate life's rocky, terrains,
Though brittle and wobbly; just come!

Come, rise up and let's share the lovely
Dawn, as she inspires yet another day;
Slowly, infusing life with hopefulness,
She soothes all bitterness; just come!

Come, let your wrinkled brow bring smiles
That can brighten up the darkened world,
And promising possibilities on life's pages;
Unsure as you are, why not? Just come!

Come today, for tomorrow never comes;
Being today, yesterday or the day ahead.
Why do you wait in this ephemeral space,
Memory laden, and shaken? Just come!

Working Woman

She wakes up alone, before the crack of dawn,
For she's been thinking, planning, and worrying
About the children to feed, things they'll need,
As they sleep; snoring, without a care showing.

She tosses and turns, gets up to light the boiler,
That'll later inspire little lives in blissful dreams;
Now playing with angels in their sleeping reverie,
As they toss and turn, chasing colourful candies.

Smiling, as she spies on their sweet innocence,
She's encouraged to fight for her family progress;
From present state of lack, poverty, and distress,
Which alone, she is fighting, battling to redress.

School uniforms at the ready, so she fries bakes
To fill bellies with tea, and keep hunger at bay,
Then promises them more, later at dinner-time;
Though the welfare support is nowhere in sight!

Bravely dignified, she reminds parting children
Of their duty; to aspire to heights that'll remedy
Her heavy-heartedness: smiling, she kisses them,
Rekindling confidence and strength to carry on.

Hidden sighs mean later will take care of itself,
So will tomorrow: then puts on her long coat.
After sipping a last mouthful of hot black tea,
Prepares to smile at work, with bakes for lunch!

Blessings

Don't compare your own soul with another man's soul,
In case it's bound for hell, while heaven awaits yours;
Take each breath with gratitude; luckily, you breathe,
Because someone's maybe struggling for their very last.
Don't complain when sunshine overheats the earth,
For as snow brings chaos, many curse their rotten lot.

Teach those who say their own land has little wealth,
To stop complaining and give thanks for their health;
For in *rich* States, gun/knife crimes mock life's power.
Take pride in your skin - that enviable shade or colour;
Many endure near-death punishments of heated degrees
Relentlessly: and discover only few eyes will be pleased.

Eat the natural products of the soil with thankfulness,
It's not *poor* food; in *rich* places some die from its lack.
Don't bemoan the many past 'friends' that you've lost,
Destiny replaces her 'helpers' with the 'killers' who flew.
Remember, the grass is only greener on the other side
Because of how you perceive the shade of green there.

For the humble, grateful, birds of the sky eat and freely fly;
But filled with greed, man rejects the blessings he receives.

Imagine this!

Imagine this!
A chance / for morality / philosophy / and / sustainability!
Imagine this / living in a world / where climate / is no longer
changing / or risking / destruction. / Can you / Imagine this!
A world / not shaking/ from rampant / disease / conspiracies.
Where the poor / and hungry / no longer /sleep / in the cold,
And there is / justice / peace / love / changes / for the better.
A world / where /I'm free / to be me / despite / differences.
Where / stereotype / and stigmatise/ no longer / cause offences.

Imagine this / a world / where black lives / do matter/ equally;
Totally / free / from stagnation / and skin colour / is never / the
measure / of your life's / worth / nor / the place / of your birth.
Imagine this / a world where / everyone's free / can eat / not
Dying / from war / hunger / starvation / or unilateral / power.
Imagine this / world / where people / have / the will to share
the earth's / resources / fairly / destroying / all wealth barriers.

Imagine this / world / where/ humankind / is brave / enough
to stamp out / destruction / from tantrum-throwing / boys / in
suits / dressed up / as men / too ashamed / to admit / they don't
have / the answers / to the world's / problems / they've created.
Imagine this / united / people / determined / to abolish / hate
Inspire / freedom / from insecurities / struggles / violence / fear;
Brave enough / to begin / instigating / healing / the / human race.
Imagine this / visionary people / rising together / together / rising!
Rising up / You / Me / We / no stigmatise / or stereotype / *Protopia!
Imagine This! *Protopia - See Glossary*

The Breeze Calls

Here, in my favourite spot is where I now lie,
Looking up at the clear, cloudless blue sky;
I'm sweating in the sticky, sweltering sun,
As the cool, calm, tropical breeze calls me.....

Amongst many stumpy cocoa trees laden with
Their pinkish-purple and yellowy-green pods,
Hugged by trails of climbing water-melon vines,
The humid heat empties his sizzling degrees
On the thirsty, parched trees, as they dance
Playfully, wishing the nearby whistling ravine,
Gurgling in her free-flowing watery splendour,
Would bathe them with her long, cool wetness.

Sniffing air, I'm drunk with habitual happiness,
As the breeze calls, spreading familiar petrichor
Of the scorching sunny surroundings, I listen
To the peace and serenity of this favourite spot.
Enveloped with a fortuitous fulfilling feeling
Of calm, I sigh noisily, at stillness which do not
Speak back to me with words, so I must find
Ways to capture this placid perfection forever.

.....Locked in this moment in time, is a memory of
Indelible recollection of tropical climate friends;
The blue cerulean sky, the stifling heat, protective
Trees, a babbling brook, a past moment in time -
A memorized picture of this land to last a lifetime:
And just as the breeze sought my attention then,
It's cool calmness will call me again to this spot,
Where I will sit and listen to its call once more.

Vive Le Spirit [1]Anancy: The Bridge-Builder!

He answered the call: of all the creations in the world,
[2]Nyame chose god Ananse, to go as spider undercover.
Armed with great mission, the smartest of all, hide
Inside slave-ship to the Caribbean as wisdom incognito.

Have you heard about Ananse, the trickster spider
Who speaks all languages and dialects of the world?
Master of [3]*Crick-Crack* stories, taught hidden wisdom
To slaves who outsmarted colonials on Plantations?

He rode the waves with screaming slaves on ships,
Sailed Atlantic ocean: to prevent total destruction
Among his people: mission, healing hurt in new land,
Though things did fall apart; knew they'd overcome.

Filled with pride, great resolve, reflecting, reminding,
Unity in spirit, one love: he witnessed the singing
Of women with head-ties and best frocks dancing,
And men displaying[4] Kalinda and [5]Kumina, as braves.

Keeping practices that's theirs, honouring traditions,
Ancestors sent blessings when they were awakened;
Talking drums gave way to [6]tamboo-bamboo bands,
As they preserved [7]Shango and [8]Papa Legba secrets.

He carried enough wisdom in his eight arms and legs,
To make sure he spread African wisdom everywhere.
So if you feeling really smart, it's Anancy inside you.
If you hear good wisdom listen; then take it home!

If you feel like dancing in the old time-honoured way,
Or want to *write* stories, in a new Anancy Tradition,
Pass on the *Crick-Crack* stories, till you overcome;
Because that Anancy's spirit; it's still making it so!

See Glossary

1. *Anancy*
2. *Nyame*
3. *Crick Crack storytelling*
4. *Kalinda*
5. *Kumina*
6. *Tamboo-bamboo*
7. *Shangoo*
8. *Papa Legba*

GLOSSARY

Introduction – (page i-x)

Roselle & Friends Talk Show – a weekly Magazine-style show on Sky Channel 589, each Wednesday 11.30am, presented and produced by Roselle Thompson

Echoes of Memory – (page 1)

1. *force-ripe* – (usually refers to fruit): here means precocious, especially sexually
2. *Limacol* – a soothing refreshing mentholated eau de toilette, with fresh lime fragrance, used widely by Caribbean people.
3. *Shango* – a Caribbean Orisha, developed from Afro-Caribbean syncretic religions; originally a deity in Yoruba religion from West Africa.
4. *tamboo-bamboo* – the precursor to the steel pan music in the Caribbean the tamboo-bamboo was a percussion instrument created in the Caribbean, made from various length of bamboo sticks, that were played in ensembles called tamboo-bamboo bands. Its name derives from the French word for drum and the material that the instrument is made from. When pounded on the ground the bamboo sticks produced sounds comparable to the hand drum.
5. *Merenge* - a Caribbean style of music and dance, typically in duple and triple time, from Dominica.
6. *Spouge* - a style of Barbadian popular music It is primarily a fusion of Jamaican ska with Trinidadian calypso
7. *Kaiso* is a type of music popular in Trinidad and Tobago, and other countries, especially of the Caribbean, such as Grenada, Belize, Barbados, St. Lucia, and Dominica, which originated in West Africa, and later evolved into calypso music.
8. *Cadence* - a dance music and modern méringue popularized in the Caribbean
9. *Quadrille* – a French-Caribbean folk dance in the Caribbean, and also the music of Martinique.

Tropical Sunrise Sea – (page 3)

1. **Triangle** – referring to the **Slave Triangle** – the sailing route taken by British slave traders between 1532 and 1832, carrying trade goods, set sail from Britain, bound for West Africa. From there 12 million African people were enslaved and taken to the Americas and the Caribbean to work on plantations.
2. **Zepingue tremblant,** (Caribbean French-Creole language); translated means *'trembling pins of gold,'* but recognised as embroidery and lace in the type of dress worn in by-gone days, in the Caribbean.
3. **fête (n) fêting (v)** - In Trinidad and Tobago and other English-speaking Caribbean territories, fêtes are huge parties held outdoors, with loud music, food, dancing, and lots to eat and drink.

Education Fail – (page 13)

*****Su-su Hand** - A *susu* or *sou-sou* or *'"asue,"'* (also known as a merry-go-round), is a type of informal savings club arranged between a small group of people. Each person pays an agreed fixed sum of money on a periodic basis (weekly or monthly) and at that time, one member of the group takes all the money that has been paid (their share or ***"Hand"***), until everyone has a turn. It is also called ***"Pardna"*** in Jamaica, ***"Box Hand"*** in Guyana, and ***Conubite*** in Haiti. The name ***"susu"*** has been traced to Yoruba, ***osusu***, in West Africa.

Elvira's Soul – (page 14)

1. **La Diablese** - Known as a devil woman, **La Diablese** is a Caribbean folktale, of a woman whose beautiful figure and dress make her extremely attractive. She wears a large, brimmed hat to hide her disfigured and ugly face, and it is said that one of her legs is cloven hoofed (e.g. she has a cow leg). She appears on nights when its full moon; waiting in remote places, on highways, where a man is likely to pass. She often hides behind trees and casts spells on her unsuspecting male victims, leading them into the forest for sexual favours. Then the victims find themselves lost, confused, and often come to a terrible end.
2. **Frankenstein** – One of the characters in Marry Shelley's 1818 gothic novella. **Victor Frankenstein** is the main character who, after studying chemical processes and the decay of living beings,

gains an insight into the creation of life and gives life to his own creature; a monster.
3. ***Jekyll & Hyde*** (or *The Strange Case of Dr Jekyll and Mr. Hyde*) is a gothic novella, written by Robert Louis Stevenson in 1886, is about Dr Henry Jekyll, a Victorian gentleman, who occasionally battles between the good and evil within himself, leading to the struggle between his dual personalities as both Henry Jekyll and Edward Hyde. He spends a great part of his life trying to repress the evil urges within him, (personified as Mr. Hyde).

Still Birth – (page 35)

1. ***Mulatto breed*** – used in slavery times to mean the first generation offspring of a European white and a black African parent. The original word comes from Spanish and Portuguese **(*Mulattas*), meaning a cross-breed of a donkey and a horse – a mule.** Fairly dated now as it has been replaced by other offensive descriptions e.g. half-caste, mixed race.
2. ***Seven Powers*** – refers to **The Seven African Powers.** They are the seven Orishas that are called upon in times of need. The phrase **Seven African Powers** is found in various religions, including Santeria, Hoodoo/Voodoo, Candomble, and Arara. In Spanish, the phrase translates to *Siete Potencias*, or seven powers. The Orishas that make up the Seven African Powers are: ***Elegua, Yemaya, Oshun, Chango, Obatala, Oya,*** and ***Ogun.***
3. ***Legba or (Elegua in W. Africa),*** is one of many West African and Caribbean Vodoo gods or "Loas." He is called the *Lord of the Crossroads,* since he serves as an intermediary between man and the spirit world. He is petitioned in matters of destiny and fate.
4. ***Si ilekun fun mi*** is Yoruba and translated in English means, **"open the door for me."**

Loki's Return – (page 37)

Loki, the god of chaos, is a very famous example of a Trickster character. This shape-shifting, trouble-making god is constantly on the look-out for a way to undermine authority figures. Loki is famous for his dangerous charisma and his wicked sense of humour. He uses his way with words, to ingratiate himself with powerful women, only to set their hearts against people he doesn't like. Not only does Loki run amuck of the social rules of culture, but he also defies the rules of nature.

1. Refers to George Orwell's Allegorical novella entitled ***Animal Farm***, which was first published in 1945. The book tells the story of a group of farm animals who rebel against their human farmer, hoping to create a society where the animals can be equal, free, and happy. However, the rebellion is betrayed, and the farm ends up in a bad state as it was before; led by a dictator pig called Napoleon.

Soucouyant – (page 45)
The ***soucouyant***, also known as the ***lagaroo, Ole Higue,*** and ***loogaroo***, is a woman by day, but in the night, she can shed her skin and transform into a fireball. In this form, she flies and feeds off of the blood of other animals, human and non-human. This is a very popular character and there are many different versions about her origin and behaviour in the Caribbean region.

Ciara's Costly Catastrophe – (page 47)
Storm Ciara was an extratropical cyclone European windstorm, named on February 5 before impacting the UK and Ireland on February 8 to 9. Heavy rains and gusts of wind reaching more than 90mph brought widespread flooding and travel disruptions, as Storm Ciara hit the UK. Trees were topped, buildings were damaged, and some homes had to be evacuated as rivers burst their banks.

A Voice of Our Own – (page 60)
1. In ***History of the Voice: The Development of Nation Language in Anglophone Caribbean Poetry***, Kamau Brathwaite discusses the differences between English and languages in the Caribbean, states that although we in the Caribbean have plurality; meaning an input of imperial languages from colonialists – French, Dutch, Spanish and a mixture of English which resulted in a nation language that was spoken by those who were brought into the Caribbean (language of slaves, labourers, servants etc). However, he takes the idea of a nation language beyond the simple merging of two linguistic systems and instead incorporates a much wider variety of linguistic variation to include vestiges of the Amerindian, a number of African languages, Hindi, Chinese which share semantics and syntactical features. (*Voice* 6-7)

2. Roselle Thompson in *Understanding the Development of Caribbean Orature: A Fusion of Oral and Literary Traditions* (Unpublished MPhil Thesis 2006; some 20 years post Brathwaite's *History of the Voice* 1984), argues that Caribbean Oral Traditions and their interactive impact on European literary models imposed on the Caribbean region have produced a fusion of genres, identified as **Caribbean Orature:** syncretised via a Creolisation process, which incorporates Words as printed text, spoken word, performance, music, film, and dance. These highlight generically fused characteristics that are unavoidably linked to auditory, visual, rhythmic, dramatic, electronic, technology, media, tonal and scribal elements in Caribbean literary praxis.

Imagine This - (page 82)
**Protopia* is a state that means better today than yesterday. It is much harder to visualise because it contains new benefits with inherent new problems, and a complex interaction of working. However, the potential brokenness is harder to predict.

Protopian progress in the world so far, describes achievements over several centuries e.g. the abolishment of slavery, the end of the death penalty, civil rights and liberties, universal suffrage, animal rights, same sex marriage, the attenuation of war, signalling the oscillation of nuclear war in maintaining worldwide human security; all taking place one small step at a time.

Vive Le Spirit Anancy: The Bridge-Builder – (page 84)
1. *Anancy/Ananse* – The tale of Anancy is a direct transfer from West Africa to the Caribbean. It is the most popular of all the African folktales that were taken to the Caribbean via the slaves. It originates from the Akan people of present day Ghana, the original name being Kwaku Ananse. The name Ananse is an Ashanti word which means "spider".
2. *Nyame* (or *Nyambe, Nyankopon*) is the Sky deity of the Akan people of Akanland (South Ghana), the leader of the Abosom, the Akan spirits and minor gods. His name means "he who knows and sees everything" and "omniscient, omnipotent sky god" in the Akan language; and "he who does not speak" in the Luyana language.

3. ***Crick-Crack storytelling*** – This African folk tale tradition is well-known and practised within the Caribbean territories. Some vary in renditions, and in some islands like St. Lucia, it is performed in French Creole or Patois language.
4. ***Kalinda*** – or *Kalenda/Caleinda/Calinda/Corlinda/Kalenda* – in Trinidad began as a combative stick-fighting ritual which transformed into a dance to the drum and a shack-shack in the plantations during colonial times.
5. ***Kumina*** – can be described as one of the most African religious expression in the Caribbean, with its roots originating from the Congo region of Central Africa.
6. ***Tamboo-bamboo*** – the precursor to the steel pan music in the Caribbean the tamboo-bamboo was a percussion instrument created in the Caribbean, made from various length of bamboo sticks, that were played in ensembles called tamboo bamboo bands
7. ***Shango*** – a Caribbean Orisha, developed from Afro-Caribbean syncretic religions; originally a deity in Yoruba religion from West Africa.
8. ***Papa Legba, Legba or (Elegua in W. Africa)***, is one of many West African and Caribbean Vodoo gods or "Loas." He is called the *Lord of the Crossroads,* since he serves as an intermediary between man and the spirit world.

www.ingramcontent.com/pod-product-compliance
Lightning Source LLC
Chambersburg PA
CBHW031546080526
44588CB00018B/2713